the
NATURE of
LANGUAGE

A SHORT GUIDE TO WHAT'S IN OUR HEADS

Bill VanPatten

Graphic Design by Paintbox Creative

ISBN: 978-1-942544-68-5
© 2019, ACTFL
1001 North Farifax Street, Suite 200
Alexandria, VA 22314

ACKNOWLEDGEMENTS

I could not write these acknowledgments without thanking all of the great linguists over the years who have educated me in one way or another. Some of these include Noam Chomsky, Ray Jackendoff, Karen Zagona, Andrew Radford, and Cedric Boeckx. And, of course, I am indebted to all of my professors in graduate school who got me started in this wonderful world of the scientific study of language.

I would also like to give shout-outs to those working in second-language acquisition from a linguistic perspective, as they have influenced me in more ways than they may know: Lydia White, Jason Rothman, Silvina Montrul, Roumyana Slabakova, Michael Sharwood Smith, Roger Hawkins, Bonnie Schwartz, and many others.

Finally, my thanks go to the folks at ACTFL: Howie Berman, Paul Sandrock, and especially Meg Malone—the "bestest" editor an author could have. Thanks also to Todd Larson for his expert copy editing and the reviewers who offered thoughtful suggestions about the first draft.

*For all language teachers who are striving
to do something other than what's in textbooks,
and for anyone else who marvels at the human mind.*

TABLE OF CONTENTS

Prologue

How I Got Started in All This

I am fascinated by language. It is the one thing that most clearly separates us from the rest of the animal and plant kingdoms. I consider myself fortunate to have made a career in the language sciences, or "linguistics." I fell into the language sciences by accident. As a gay Latino kid who was shy and withdrawn from being bullied and having such an unhappy childhood, I retreated into the world of science. I loved chemistry. For my eighth birthday I prodded my mother into buying me one of those children's chemistry sets. I spent more time mixing chemicals and running experiments in my closet-sized bedroom than doing anything else. I studied the Periodic Table of Elements, and I drew molecules for different compounds, in an effort to understand how chemical bonds worked. In high school I discovered physics, and I still read about that discipline today in my limited spare time. (The quantum world is fascinating, but it remains tough for me.) I even dated a physicist once, but that's really not important to the story here.

Then, in college, something happened to me that turned me away from pursuing any kind of science as a discipline. First, I came out of my shell and blossomed into the outgoing radio-show host many people know me as. (I'm still shy, but one-on-one shy. I'm not shy in a big crowd, as some of you know. Put me on stage, and I'm fine. Fix me up on a date, and I'm tongue-tied. Again, not important to the story here, but it makes for some good background.)

Second, I didn't fit in with other chemistry kids, and I just couldn't get fired up about chemistry anymore. So I wound up with majors in Political Science and Spanish—the latter because of my own upbringing in a bicultural, bilingual world. Then, something happened I couldn't have expected. As I continued to grow and wanted to get away from my family (yep, there's more to the story there), I left California and went to graduate school in Texas to pursue Latin American Studies. I had a teaching assistantship in Spanish to pay for my basic living, but mid-way through the first semester of grad school I realized I'd made a mistake. Latin American Studies weren't doing it for me. I considered moving back to California when one day a Spanish professor said to me, "You seem to have a scientific mind. Have you tried linguistics?" I'd never heard of linguistics, but he convinced me not to go back to California and to remain in Texas to pursue a Master of Arts in Hispanic Linguistics. Well, I did, and the rest is history. I became a language scientist.

And Then There Was Acquisition and Teaching

But I was also interested in both language acquisition and language teaching. How I got into that is another story. Let's just say some other professors and mentors saw something in me, and the next thing I knew I was not just a language scientist but a language educator. And here I am now, talking about language to other language educators—and I enjoy talking to teachers. I regularly give workshops, talks, and lectures on language acquisition and language teaching. Over the years I have discovered that the nature of language is the best-kept secret from language teachers, just as it had been from me as an undergraduate. Sounds wrong, right? I mean, shouldn't language teachers be keenly aware of the nature of language? After all, language is the object of acquisition.

My guess is that one reason why teachers tend not to study the nature of language is that teacher education tends to treat language like any other subject matter. That is, to teach Spanish and French, for example, you needn't know about language in general; you just need to know Spanish and French (e.g., have a major in it). Textbooks will provide you with what you need to teach, and principles of education take care of the rest. This is certainly true for learning *about* language, the same way you might learn about history or Shakespeare. In this scenario, language teacher education is not seen as anything different from social studies teacher education or English teacher education.

But what if the goals are to acquire language and learn to communicate? Acquisition and communication do not fall out of knowing about language as subject matter. When acquisition and communication become goals of language classes, the need for teachers to know about the nature of language takes on new importance. I won't say why here; I'm hoping it will become clear as you read this book. I will suggest this now, though: *Knowing about the nature of language is one of the keys for releasing teachers from the lockstep curricula built around current textbooks.* For teachers who really want to teach for acquisition, communicative ability and proficiency, knowing something about how language actually works can be liberating. It can provide teachers with important arguments for striking out on their own and exploring new methods and alternative curricula and assessments.

Is This Book Just for Language Teachers?

Because of my background and my belief that language teachers can benefit from an understanding of the nature of language, most of my comments are directed to educators. But as I reflect, just about anyone can read this book and gain some insight into the nature of language (except for the last chapter). So, although I tend to speak to language teachers throughout this book, I hope to have written in a style accessible to a broad group of non-experts: administrators, parents, students, people browsing the shelves at Barnes & Noble (assuming people still do this), and others. After all, very few of us leave formal education with any real understanding about what's in our heads when it comes to language. We tend to think of language as what our grammar teachers taught us or what we read in, for example, *The Idiot's Guide to English* (a terrible title, but there you are). As I hope this book will show, language is much more abstract and complex than these sources suggest.

So if you're a language teacher, I'm glad to see you here. And spread the word: maybe someone who's not a language educator would like to read this book as well.

Some Caveats

Let me offer a few words of warning before you delve into this book. At times I will purposefully challenge you. You may feel as if I am yanking the rug out from under you or that what you've learned about Spanish, French, German or Russian doesn't amount to a hill of beans. Please don't think I mean to diminish your background. Instead, my goal is to open the door to a new way of looking at the world around you. There might be, in these pages, something that can put you on a new path—something that pushes you to look at language and language learning in new ways.

You also might feel that I am occasionally deriding textbooks, especially when I say that the rules and patterns they present aren't psychologically real. I'm not faulting textbooks or authors for the content of textbooks. The shape and content of language textbooks is due to historical inertia, but publishers and authors are simply doing what's expected of them. So think of my comments about textbooks as this: maybe there's a new way to conceive of textbooks. Maybe there's a new content for language textbooks. Maybe you can have different expectations about textbooks, and then these expectations are passed on to publishers and authors. Textbooks can be our best friends, if they actually embody the goals we have for our language learners and are informed by the nature of language and language acquisition.

Because this is a brief book meant to be (highly) introductory, at times you will see me apologize to my linguistics colleagues for taking shortcuts in presenting some facts about language. These shortcuts are necessary and desirable to drive home the main points in this book. Rest assured, fellow language scientists, I'm well aware of the bigger and even more complicated and abstract picture than what I present on these pages.

Oh, and one more detail, as long as we're on the topic of linguistics: When you see an asterisk in front of a sentence, that means the sentence is not possible in a given language (asterisks are how linguists indicate something wrong). So, for example, *Bill repainted his office* is a possible sentence, but *Bill rewoke up this morning* is not.

Finally, to keep this book short, I focus largely on sentence structure, with some word structure thrown in. Occasionally I refer to sounds and meaning. This book just doesn't have enough space to cover what language is in its totality. But, even with the book's limited focus, you should get a good idea that all aspects of language can be discussed the same way. Besides, I also wanted to focus on what teachers and textbooks typically call "grammar." Be aware, too, that I am a "generativist" and "psycholinguist" by training and education. I take a particular perspective on language not only because it is my background, but also because I believe that the perspectives underlying the ideas in this book are on the right track to talk about what's in the human mind.

Other perspectives on the nature of language are out there, but no matter which one you take, you can't avoid the basic ideas underlying this book: *What we think of as rules and patterns just aren't psychologically real.* I will occasionally refer to other approaches, but, again, this book is purposefully (and for some, mercifully) short. I will urge those working in other frameworks to make their own case about the nature of language, but once more, in the end, we tend to agree on the basic idea of this book: *Language isn't what most people think it is.*

And, to be sure, I want everyone to know that the title of this book is purposeful: *The Nature of Language: A Short Guide to What's in Our Heads.* It is not a book about language use, communication, how people speak, how to teach language, or what to teach. It is what its title says: a glimpse of the abstract and complex mental representation we call language. If you're wondering why you should read this book, I hope it will become clear by the end. It is not long, so, hopefully, when you get to the final chapter, you'll say to yourself "I get it…" And, just in case, I make it salient there.

As I complete this manuscript in early 2019 and contemplate retirement (gulp!) or something else (double gulp!), I still marvel at the nature of language and the human capacity to acquire such an abstract, complex system. I haven't lost the awe I had experienced way back when I took my first courses in linguistics. I've had a great career, and I've been able to move back and forth among linguistics, language acquisition, and language teaching, thanks to readers like you. So I offer you my heartfelt gratitude for inspiring me to write this book. I hope you enjoy this short, nifty guide to the nature of language and what's in our heads.

Bill VanPatten
Chowchilla, California
January 2019

Chapter 1

Some Preliminaries

I want to begin this chapter with a simple yet provocative idea: *Language textbooks are not a particularly good place to get insights into the nature of language.* This may sound odd coming from someone like me. After all, the author of best-selling university-level language textbooks in Spanish and French shouldn't say those things, right? What's more, the claim is shocking for most teachers, because the textbook industry is a major one in education, and how could textbooks not be good places to get insights into the nature of language? But the truth of the matter is, commercially produced language textbooks can't capture the nature of language, for a variety of reasons. For one thing, language courses aren't linguistics courses, and no Spanish Level 1 student wants to learn about such things as verb internal versus verb external subjects, perfectivity and aspect, phrase structure and head directionality. (We will go into some detail on abstract concepts in Chapter 2.)

In addition, language textbooks are built on tradition. For decades and decades, they have presented language in a particular way, and that's what teachers (and students) expect. Furthermore, teachers are just not trained or educated in the nature of language. It's not part of professional development or the baccalaureate experience, so teachers tend to look in textbooks for things they've already seen in, well, textbooks. And if it's on Page 32 of the textbook, it must be something real, right?

What's more, the Internet is not a particularly good place to learn about the nature of language either, unless you look up articles on, say, linguistic theory and language processing. Like textbooks, websites for teachers and students provide inaccurate descriptions and rules that don't represent what winds up in someone's head.

So I'm going to challenge you, the reader, to jettison some of your basic ideas about language—ideas you likely got from textbooks, "methods" classes and Google searches. Forget what you may have learned from these sources if you want to understand what language really is—any language, not just the one you teach. To help you do this, we're going to start this book with some very common, frequently used ideas in language teaching and discuss how they are neither accurate portrayals of language nor particularly useful for acquisition. This is necessary because, to understand language acquisition and any implications it has for language teaching, we need to know what the object of language acquisition is—that is, what language is.

Are you ready to be challenged? Because we're starting with what language isn't, I will focus on what I believe to be four of the most commonly used terms or phrases in teaching and among non-linguists such as administrators, parents, students, and browsers at Barnes & Noble.

Before you go on. . .

Think about your own education for language teaching. You might have majored in a particular language and studied its literatures and cultures. You might have pursued an education degree in which you studied curriculum development, educational psychology, and the history of education, for example. What percentage of time in all of these courses did you actually study and discuss "the nature of language"? (We're not talking about "advanced grammar" courses you might have taken as part of your major.)

Patterns

I regularly hear teachers talk about "language patterns." They tell me, for example, that they do such-and-such in the language classroom to help their students "see the patterns" or "notice the patterns." Or they tell me that, to help their students, they stop and "point out the patterns." To understand what's problematic about the term "patterns," let's look at an analogy: constellations.

Have you ever looked up at the sky and seen the Big Dipper? How about Orion? Scorpio? If you have, you are looking at "patterns" of stars in the sky. This is what the ancient Babylonians claimed to have seen as they originated the classic Zodiac, which was later adopted by the Greeks. But in the 21st century, we know a lot more about stars and the universe than most ancient civilizations did. So, as we ponder constellations as patterns of stars, we see that they are illusions. Why would I say this?

The idea of constellations is possible only if you perceive them as patterns against a flat, dark sky. You can take a sheet of black construction paper, poke holes in it to form an image of the Big Dipper, and hold it up with light behind it. *Presto!* You've recreated a constellation. But stars aren't pinpricks of light against a flat background. Space is not flat. Stars (and galaxies) are scattered all over a three-dimensional universe, and some may not even be close to each other. They merely *resemble* pinpricks against a flat sky to us. For example, two of the main stars in Orion—Betelgeuse and Rigel—are so far apart in real space it would take about four hundred years to travel from one to the other at the speed of light. (If you don't know the distance of a light-year, it's about 5.88 trillion miles, so Betelguese and Rigel are about 400 × 5.88 trillion miles apart.) If you traveled several hundred light-years into space, you wouldn't even see Orion, because the position of the stars would look different from your vantage point—or at best you might see a "warped" version of Orion. Those stars might look like a cat, an oyster, or a flat line.

In short, stars and galaxies exist in three-dimensional space, but we perceive constellations in two-dimensional space from Earth. When our ancestors looked up into the sky and saw those stars, they may not have understood what space really was (but maybe some did). In a certain sense, we are just like our ancestors every time we look up and fail to remind ourselves that those patterns don't exist: we have imposed them onto what our eyes take in.

So-called language patterns are similar. They are illusions, in that they are our interpretations of what our eyes (and ears) take in, but are no more real than constellations. We impose patterns on what we perceive, but what is actually there is not the pattern at all. A linguist is like an astronomer: with the telescope of linguistic inquiry, the linguist can look beyond a pattern to see what is really going on with language and why it looks like a pattern to the non-expert.

Kind of heavy, right?

> Patterns are an illusion. We impose patterns on what we perceive, but what is actually there might be quite different from what we see.

One more thing about patterns: the term "language patterns" was used by pre-acquisition-era people, that is, those in that era of our academic history before we began to gather empirical data on both first and second-language acquisition. The "acquisition era" started in the 1960s for first language and in the 1970s for second language, so let's establish "pre-acquisition" as prior to 1970. Before then, language learning was dominated by structural linguistics and behaviorism. Structural linguists sought patterns in the language, and those patterns became what behaviorists interpreted as habits to be learned.

For those of you who don't remember or know much about the pre-acquisition era of language teaching, behaviorism was a psychological theory claiming that all behaviors were habits learned through conditioning. Conditioning basically comprised a response-feedback system in which a person's particular behavior or pattern was somehow rewarded, not rewarded, or punished. Behaviorists saw language as a set of habits or patterns to be learned this way. This was translated into audiolingualism as the "scientific" approach to teaching languages. Audiolingualism comprised memorization of dialogues, practice via drills, and other non-meaningful activities. With the revolution of linguistics in the 1960s and the dawn of the acquisition era, both structural linguistics and behaviorism fell to the wayside. Yet teachers and non-experts still refer to "language patterns." In a real sense, then, the use of this term is an outdated throwback to the pre-acquisition era. When we talk about language patterns, we are subtly invoking an outmoded way of thinking about language, language acquisition, and, by extension, language instruction.

Before you go on. . .

The 1960s saw a real revolution in language science. Linguistics was turned on its head with Chomsky's basic ideas about "a generative linguistic system." Those ideas still drive current linguistic theory, although the theory itself has evolved. Simultaneously, we began to see the first empirical research on first-language acquisition that showed it could not be the result of habit and pattern learning as suggested by behaviorism. And in the early 1970s, we saw the birth of empirical research on second-language acquisition. Yet many of the basic ideas about language and language acquisition remain unknown to many language *(cont.)*

teachers, and to the public more generally. Do you think this typifies "scientific revolutions"? Can you think of other things you've heard about in your formal studies that haven't made it to "common knowledge"? Can you think of some scientific revolutions that have significantly affected common knowledge? Can you think of some scientific revolutions that have been misinterpreted or are not well understood?

Rules

Related to patterns is the idea of rules. Verbs must agree with their subjects in Spanish and Russian. Most Japanese and Latin nouns (actually, noun phrases) must be marked for case. A conjugated verb in German and Swedish is always in "second position" in a simple sentence or in a main clause. These and other rules populate textbooks and are the bane of many students who try to memorize, practice and take tests on them.

Before we examine why rules, like patterns, are not psychologically real, let's remember where the idea of such rules came from. Before institutionalized education, language rules were nonexistent. Pre-literate tribes worldwide learned other languages through contact without such rules. For example, there was contact among Native American tribes in North America long before the Europeans came, and some tribal members learned another tribe's language. (For the record, not all indigenous tribes in North America were pre-literate.) Phoenician was widely spoken as a second language in the ancient Mediterranean area, although no formal educational system existed anywhere; there was no such thing as Phoenician 101. I conducted research to learn when the first language textbook with rules in it was published but was unsuccessful. We know, however, that Greeks developed "grammar" books to help people improve their writing and to read Homer, for example. And both Romans and Greeks used "readers" (which hardly resembled our current textbooks) to learn each other's languages. By medieval times, there were books for learning Latin and Greek in educational settings, and children who entered what was actually called "grammar school" learned Latin via memorization of rules,

> *Rules aren't actually rules but external descriptions of what we can't talk about or don't know how to talk about.*

declensions, conjugations, and translation. Once rules appeared in a textbook, they became sacred to language teaching and have been in use ever since.

So what's wrong with rules such as "verbs and subjects must agree in Spanish" and in German "the conjugated verb appears in second position in a simple or main clause"? Like patterns, rules are illusions. They are our perceptions of the "surface" of language and, like constellations, are real only because we can't perceive language in some other way. Now, let's be honest. It surely does seem as if verbs and subjects agree in Spanish, because a sentence like *Mis padres habla español* ("My parents speak Spanish") is simply not a good sentence. (Remember, an asterisk indicates that a sentence is not possible in a given language.) The sentence must be, *Mis padres hablan español*. The question is: Do verbs agree with subjects, or is something else going on? After all, lots of languages have no verb forms that correspond with particular things (e.g., Mandarin, Japanese, much of English), indicating subject-verb agreement. And in Spanish I can start a conversation by saying *Soy profesor de lingüística* ("I'm a linguistics professor"), which has no subject for the verb to agree with, yet I must use *soy*. Could what we see as "agreement" be actually something else? We call it 'agreement' because that is what we think we see, but maybe something else is going on behind the scenes for which we don't have the words to describe.

A better way to think about rules in language teaching is that they are not rules and not psychologically real but are external descriptions of something internal we can't talk about or don't know how to talk about. Like patterns and constellations, we may be looking at something in a flat space, but there may be something deeper going on, that learners of a language eventually acquire. Not the rules in textbooks.

Before you go on. . .

Several times I have used the term "psychologically real." I mean that what we say about language is not what exists in anyone's head. Rules and such may seem "real" from our external perspective, but they are not "real" in the sense that these rules are not what resides in anyone's head. Can you think of another way to describe this situation? Can you think of a term other than "psychologically real" to talk about what's in people's heads?

This all may sound esoteric and weird, but we will offer some concrete examples in Chapter 2 and elsewhere in this book. I'm just trying to get you to a "Hmmm" moment.

Structures

The term 'structures' is similar to 'rules' and 'patterns' in that teachers often talk about learning the structures of a lan-

Language has structure but not structures.

guage. Let me say this right away: language has *structure* but not *structures*. I know your head is probably spinning from what we said about patterns and rules, so I'll try to be more concrete here as a preview to something we'll discuss in the next chapter.

'Structures' is, in essence, synonymous with 'rules' for teachers. So if rules aren't actually real (psychologically speaking), neither are structures. But language is built on *hidden structure*. Example: Languages consist of phrases. All sentences contain phrases, even one-word sentences. There are noun phrases, verb phrases, and prepositional phrases. These are the phrases you can hear, see, and sort of describe. Other types of phrases you can't necessarily see and hear, and we will see some of those in the next chapter. For now, let's note that phrases have structure. Each phrase consists of a head word (the word that gives the phrase its name) and something that follows it. So in a noun phrase such as *books on language* (i.e., *I read books on language*), *books* is the head noun, and *on language* is what we call the *complement* of the head noun. All English phrases have this same underlying structure: *head + complement.* Here are some examples:

noun phrase (= N + complement): *books + on language, horses + running in the wild, table + with wobbly legs*

prepositional phrase (= P + complement): *on + language, in + the wild, with + wobbly legs*

verb phrase (= V + complement): *read + books on language, see + horses running in the wild, fix + the table with wobbly legs*

determiner phrase (= D + complement): *the + books on language, a + student of linguistics, my + class on linguistics*

So English has an underlying structure for all phrases, and that structure is uniform: *head + complement*. All sentences are constructed from the nestling of phrases, one within the other such as [VP read [NP books [PP on [NP language]]]] in English. (This exemplifies what we mean by language having *structure*, not *structures*.) Keep this idea of phrases in mind; we will review it in more detail in Chapter 2 when we discuss French and Japanese. Then we will also see phrases we can't normally see or hear but exist nonetheless.

Phrases are critical to how sentences are formed in all languages.

Before you go on. . .

Think about snowflakes. You've probably heard (and believe) that no two snowflakes are alike. Each one is unique. This is true from an external observation. But did you know that all snowflakes obey a six-sided structure? That is, all snowflakes have six sides, and all crystals within a snowflake are hexagonal or six-sided. So, even though all snowflakes seemingly look unique, they actually all obey the same underlying structure. You have to look beyond the surface. Likewise, English, Spanish, Japanese and Classical Latin all look different on the surface. But underlying, they all have to obey phrase structure: every phrase, whether or not you see it, consists of a *head* and a *complement*. What is your reaction to this idea? How does it resemble what you've been taught, for example, about the differences among English, French, Japanese, and/or any other languages?

Paradigms

Not everyone uses the word 'paradigm' in language teaching but you do hear it. Its most common use is in the term 'verbal paradigms,' or what teachers often call 'verb charts' or 'conjugations.' For example, Spanish teachers might talk about the paradigm for present-tense verb endings like this:

	SINGULAR	PLURAL
1ST	-o/ -oy	-mos
2ND	-s	-is
3RD	-a/-e	-n

German teachers may think of the paradigm case marking on definite articles that look like this (singular only).

	MASCULINE	FEMININE	NEUTER
NOMINATIVE	der	die	das
ACCUSATIVE	den	die	das
DATIVE	dem	der	dem
GENITIVE	des	der	der

In essence, paradigms are another kind of pattern we perceive in things. Spanish, for example, has a pattern for verb endings, which we call *the person-number paradigm*. German has a pattern for case-marking on articles, which we call a *case paradigm*. Although verb endings are real in Spanish and case marking is real in German, paradigms are another example of how we talk about language that isn't the way languages exist in our heads. That is, no native or non-native speakers walk around with paradigms in their heads. These paradigms are our external shorthand way to talk about language properties we can't really see. Like the stars in a constellation, paradigms are our perception of what we see in the flat space before us.

Yep, we're back to constellations again.

As we will see in the next chapter, verb endings and case marking don't exist independently of their accompanying verbs, nouns or articles. What people actually have in their heads are thousands of examples of verbs with endings on them and thousands of examples of articles with case marking. That is, in the mind of a Spanish speaker, there is no *–o* that awaits use with verbs. Instead, there are loads of verbs such as *como, vivo, ando, monto, me levanto, duermo,* and so on, all encoded with their meanings. When we hear and use language, we activate these verbs as is, or we "peel off" the *–o* to use it with made-up verbs, new verbs that enter into the language, and so on. We will discuss this further in the next chapter; for now, keep in mind that, like patterns, rules, and structures, paradigms aren't psychologically real. They're another thing we impose on language based on our external perceptions.

So What is Language?

In the previous sections we've explored typical ways people talk about language, in order to show what language is not. What *is* language, then? The exact nature of language can vary depending on what experts you talk to. I take a generative perspective on language, which is the dominant theory of language at this time and has been since the 1970s. There are other approaches, but in the end most consist of constructs and ideas that coalesce around four fundamental properties:

1. Language is mental representation.
2. Language is abstract.
3. Language is complex.
4. Language is implicit.

Let's begin with language as mental representation, that is, language exists in your head. Somewhere, somehow, it is stored as some kind of representation. As such, language is not what many teachers and non-experts mean when they say, for instance, "Watch your language!" Because language is mental representation, it is not the same thing as language use in communication. Communication is the expression and interpretation of meaning in a given context for a given purpose. But communication is not language, and language is not communication. Communication may make use of language (among humans), but it is not the same thing as language.

> Because language is mental representation, it is not the same thing as communication.

As is well known, many species communicate. Bees dance. Dogs wag tails. Owls hoot. Crickets chirp. But none of these are examples of language, because of points 2 and 3 above, which we will explore in other chapters. The point is: when people say, for example, "Watch your language!" they are commenting not on your mental representation but your communication—the meaning you are expressing at a particular point in time and how you express it.

We call language mental representation also because you have "language stuff" in your head that never makes it through your lips or fingers yet is there. We can only "see it" if we probe your representation. Here are some examples (and we will see many more in subsequent chapters). If you are reading this book, you are a speaker of English, as a first or subsequent language, and should be able to tell me which of these sentences sounds weird, off, or just plain bad:

(1) Jaime didn't like the color he used, so he repainted the office.

(2) Jaime didn't like the way the cake turned out, so he rebaked it.

If you are a typical speaker of English, you should say, "(1) sounds fine, but (2) sounds odd." Why does the second one sound odd? Because "rebaked" sounds weird. English speakers might say, "Huh? You can't say 'rebaked.'" But why not? What's the so-called "rule" for using *re-* with verbs to mean to do something again? I'm pretty sure you can't tell me, but you do have mental representation for how *re-* works and doesn't work (e.g., why can't you "resleep," "rewake up," "repet a dog," "rebreak a window," or "rekiss a boyfriend"?).

You should be able to see that the following sentence is ambiguous:

(3) Jaime spied on the man with a telescope.

In this example, either the man had a telescope, or Jaime did the spying with a telescope. How did you know this sentence was ambiguous? What allows it to be ambiguous? You have mental representation for language that allows for both options.

In which of these sentences can *himself* refer to *Jaime*?

(4) Jaime showed Robert a picture of himself.

(5) Jaime understood that Robert had a picture of himself.

You probably said that only in (4) can *himself* refer to Jaime but not (5). You probably also thought that, with (4), *himself* can also refer to Robert. And if I asked you to explain why (4) can be ambiguous but not (5), you probably couldn't tell me. Am I right?

Before you go on. . .

Anthropologists, education specialists, and many who work on social issues sometimes claim that language is a social phenomenon. In this book, I *(cont.)*

claim that language is "mental stuff." Some people may conflate language and language use/communication. They believe language is only observable behavior (making it social), while people like me see language as both observable (what we see during communication or language use) and not observable (what actually exists in your head and what we have to probe to understand). What was your perspective at the outset of this chapter? Do you see language and communication as two different things? Has anything in your thoughts about language begun to change yet? If not, see if it does by the end of this book.

Here's one final example: adult speakers of English never stumble on the past tense of *drive* and almost never on its past participle. They always get it right. "He *drove* me crazy." "He's *driven* me crazy." No adult ever says, "He *drived* me crazy," or "He *has drived* me crazy." Yet, give a group of native speakers the verb "strive," and you get variation: "I *strove* to get it right." "I *strived* to get it right." "I have *striven* to get things right." "I have *strived* to get things right." Even though these two verbs have the same shape—monosyllable verbs that differ only in their initial sounds—speakers are sure about one and not the other. Where does this variation come from? Why don't the two verbs behave the same way? What allows for this behavior?

To drive the point home (the point will be *driven*, not "drived"), these examples all show that language is mental representation. Not only do we know what is possible, but we also know what is not possible, and we know when things can be ambiguous and when they can vary. I might not ever say in my entire life something like, "Jaime understood that Robert had a picture of himself," and I may never have heard this sentence before, but I can tell you immediately that *himself* can refer only to Robert in that sentence. This is why we say language is mental representation and is more than what comes off someone's lips or fingertips. There is much more to language that what most of us see daily. Yet what we see daily *and* don't see are both important parts of language and are intertwined. You can't have one without the other.

The last point brings me to a related topic: alternative approaches to this book's perspective. As the prologue mentions, I take what is called a *gener-*

> There is much more to language than what we see daily.

ative perspective inspired by the work of Noam Chomsky. But not everyone takes this perspective on language. One colleague, for example, suggested I discuss what is called *corpus linguistics,* which refers to numerical or statistical tabulations of the frequencies of words and/or phrases, specifically the contexts in which they occur. For example, the word 'résumé' combines more frequently with *my, your,* and *a,* as opposed to *the* and *any* (e.g., "Send us *your/a* résumé," but much less frequent is "Send us *the/any* résumé."). Corpus linguistics helps us to understand how language is used, which words or phrases are more frequent than others, and what tendencies people have in what they talk about. However, it isn't clear how corpus linguistics helps us to understand the real nature of language; that is, what's actually in our heads. For example, it is certainly possible to say, "Send us *any* resumé," or "Send us *the* résumé," but it is not possible to say *"Send us *an* résumé," or *"Send us résumé."

The nature of language explains why language itself behaves the way it does and what is both possible and impossible in a given language, not what people tend to say or what is more frequent in spoken or written language. The latter may be key for communication, but language and language use are not synonymous. I focus on the nature of language in this book, because many of us think that what we see in textbooks reflects the nature of language, so we try to teach that textbook content and then ask our learners to practice it.

Some people talk of language as "underlying knowledge," i.e., knowledge underlies all use of language in communication. But we must take care with the term "knowledge," because it's vague and can lead people to believe that linguistic knowledge is the same as all other knowledge. In everyday use we can talk about knowledge that's very accessible. For example, I have knowledge that if you put too much toilet paper in the bowl the toilet can plug up—and I can explain why. I have knowledge that if you don't water your lawn regularly it will turn brown—and I can explain why. And I have knowledge that if I don't put in the correct alarm code within sixty seconds after I re-enter my house, the siren will go off—and I know why. When students take non-language courses, they wind up with knowledge about history, philosophy, Shakespeare, and so on, and can talk about many concepts they've learned. But, as we will see, language as mental representation isn't so accessible. Think about examples (1)-(5) above. How accessible was the knowledge for you? You did indeed "know" something, but you couldn't explain or describe it. So I prefer to use the term "representation," although, like any language scientist, I do lapse into using "underlying knowledge" from time to time.

In addition, many of us like to say we have knowledge *about* language, but that is not the same as representation *of* language. This is where patterns, rules, and paradigms come into play. These are ways in which people try to describe the indescribable. People think they have knowledge about language when what they have are *perceptions* about the *surface* of language. For this additional reason, I use the term "mental representation" because I like to set language apart from other types of knowledge. Language is special. It's different. And it's not sets of patterns, lists of rules and structures, or paradigms. It is much more abstract. That is the topic of the next chapter.

References and Suggested Readings

Brown, R. (1973). *A first language: The early years.* Cambridge MA: Harvard University Press.

Chomsky, N. (1959). Review of Skinner's *Verbal behavior. Language, 35,* 26-58.

Pinker, S. (2007). *The language instinct.* (See especially Chapter 4, on how language works.) New York: Harper Perennial.

VanPatten, B. & Rothman, J. (2014). Against 'rules.' In A. Benati, C. Laval, & M. J. Arche (Eds.), *The grammar dimension in instructed second language acquisition: theory, research, and practice* (pp. 15-35). London: Bloomsbury.

VanPatten, B., Smith, M., Benati, A. (forthcoming). *Key questions in second language acquisition: An introduction.* Cambridge: Cambridge University Press. (See Chapter 1 on the origins of contemporary L2 research and the language science revolution of the 1960s and 1970s.)

Think About It

1. In this chapter, we have said that languages do not comprise patterns, sets of rules/structures, or paradigms, as generally conceived. But is it wrong to say that language has regularities? In one example in this chapter, we mentioned verb forms in Spanish and that all verbs referring to the speaker end in *-o* or *–oy*. This sounds like a regularity. However, are regularities and patterns the same thing? Why might it be better to say language exhibits regularities, not patterns or rules?

2. Linguistics is defined as the scientific study of language. I regularly call myself a *language scientist*. As a science, linguistics analyzes how languages behave and what their makeup is, among other things. Can you think of examples where non-scientists say or believe one concept but the science shows that concept is not what it appears to be? Here's an example: most people believe zebras are white with black stripes. But science has shown that they are actually black (or dark brown) with white stripes. Here's one more: many people think you should drink six to eight glasses of water a day. What science shows is that you should drink when you're thirsty to remain hydrated regardless of the amount.

3. Language is distinct from communication. To demonstrate, how might you communicate the following words, phrases and sentences without language?

    - "No."
    - "What are you talking about?"
    - "Wait just a minute."
    - "I'm keeping an eye on you."
    - "I don't believe what I'm hearing."

4. An idea touched on in this chapter is that there is more to language than what we can see. One major aspect of this is how we immediately know something is impossible in a language when asked. For example, I know we can contract *I* and *have* to *I've* in *I've done it*. But I immediately know that *Should I've done it?* is not a possible English sentence when someone asks me (i.e., it should have an asterisk, **Should I've done it*). Why is it not a good argument to say, "You don't like that sentence because you've never heard that combination before?"

5. Learners of English are regularly taught that you can contract the linking or auxiliary verb *be*. Here are some examples.

    a. Tom is not coming. → Tom's not coming.
    b. I am sick. → I'm sick.

You could probably come up with a "rule" for this. However, the following examples of contraction aren't possible. What's the rule?

    c. Tom's not coming, but Harry is./*Tom's not coming, but Harry's.
    d. Harry's sick, and I am too./*Harry is sick, and I'm too.

As you think about this, consider that possessives with nouns—which sound just like the contraction with is—are possible at the end of a sentence (i.e., it's not a 'sound' problem).

    e. I don't know if this is Tom's.

6. In this chapter we briefly mentioned one alternative to the generative approach to language. Below are three major approaches that talk about language differently from the way the topic is approached in this book.

- corpus linguistics
- usage-based approaches
- functional linguistics

Conduct an Internet search and review some summaries of these approaches. See if you agree with the statement in this chapter, namely, that these approaches are more about how people use language (what tendencies exist in speech and written text) rather than the nature of language itself. If you don't agree, propose a different statement.

7. In this chapter, we have reviewed why certain words and terms shouldn't be used: patterns, rules, structures, paradigms, knowledge, and others. Discuss with a friend the power of words and why we need to choose our words carefully when we talk to others. What emerges from this discussion?

Chapter 2

2

Language is Abstract

𝒯hink about these words: *email message* and *round*. If I were to ask you to label one as a concrete idea and one as an abstract idea, what would you do? Your immediate reaction is to label *email message* as concrete. You can point to one, and you can describe one, right? It's a message you type and send via a computer program such as Yahoo or Gmail. We see email messages daily. What about the word *round*? Did you have a harder time with this word? On the one hand, round things are around us all the time: grapefruits, baseballs, marbles, peas, and eyeballs (at least from the outside they look round). But if you had to describe the idea of *round,* you might get tripped up: "Well, it's something that's not square." What does "square" mean? It doesn't have any corners. What does "corners" mean? And down the rabbit hole you go trying to explain what 'round' means. You know *round* when you see it. But providing a definition or description is tough. (We'll return to this idea of *round* in Chapter 3 when discussing complexity of language.)

So *round* as an idea isn't as concrete as we think. It's much more abstract when it comes to description or definition. In this chapter, we will explore what it means for language to be abstract. To be sure, some things are concrete. For example, the difference between first-person singular and second-person singular is pretty clear. The first refers to me when I'm talking or using language, and the second refers to the person who is listening or watching me and to whom I am directing what I'm saying (or signing).

But there is much to language that is abstract, especially regarding syntax, semantics, morphology (word formation, inflections on words) and similar constructs. The best way to show how language is abstract is to start with what most people call a "rule" of language and then show how that rule doesn't capture what really goes on with language. Over the course of the chapter, we will paint a picture of just how abstract language can be. We will start with an example from Japanese so we can review phrases and introduce two different kinds of phrases. This will help us to understand the later example from French.

An Example from Japanese

Almost on the first day of learning Japanese or on the first page of any Internet site, students are told that the verb comes at the end of the sentence. So, instead of saying 'I drink coffee' in Japanese, you say:

Watashi ga kohii o nomuimasu
I   coffee drink

Instead of saying, "Taro is eating an apple," you say:

Taroo ga ringo o tabemasu
Taro   apple   eats an apple

That verbs come at the end of the sentence certainly looks right in these examples. So this rule is correct—well, sort of. Before we get into what's actually going on here, let's see what Japanese does with prepositions. Unlike English, Japanese has postpositions. So, while in English we might say, "I drink coffee at Starbucks," in Japanese we would say:

Watashi ga sutaabakkusu de kohii o nomimasu
I   Starbucks   at coffee drink

In Japanese, *de* is how we would express something like "at." Notice anything? Yes, it comes after the word for "Starbucks." This is what we mean by postposition (i.e., *de* is postposed after the noun). Now let's look at the *ga* and the *o* in the sentence. The *ga* marks the subject of the sentence, while the *o* marks the object. Notice anything? Yep. They come after the noun, just like the postpositions do. (By the way, some speakers prefer the particle *wa* instead of *ga* to mark the pronoun Watashi. They might prefer *Watashi wa kohii o nomimasu*, for example. Standard analyses by linguists claim that *ga* marks a subject when it is new information and *wa* marks a topic, which is a subject representing old information—sort of like once we mention Margaret, we don't need to repeat her name in the next sentence and can use 'she' instead as in 'Where's Margaret? She's at Starbucks'. However, after speaking with a number of linguists who focus on Japanese, I found out it appears that speakers are not uniform on this division of *ga* and *wa*.)

One final example before the big reveal: let's look at *yes/no* questions. In English, we would ask, "Do I drink coffee at Starbucks?" In Japanese, we use the particle *ka* to indicate a *yes/no* question, which looks like:.

> *Watashi ga sutsabakkusu de kohii o nomimasu ka?*
> I   Starbucks at coffee drink Q?

Hmmm. Japanese puts the particle at the end, but notice that in English our helping verb *do* winds up at the beginning of the sentence. Is something going on here? Yes—and it has to do with an abstract, deep property of languages called *phrase structure*. You may remember from Chapter 1 that language consists of phrases: noun phrases, verb phrases, prepositional phrases, and so on. These are the phrases we see and hear. We call these *lexical phrases*, because the head (nucleus) of the phrase is a lexical item. For example, the head of the noun phrase is a noun, a lexical item (e.g., *cat, dog, Bill, acquisition, coffee, Starbucks*), and the head of a prepositional phrase is a lexical item as well (e.g., *of, at, in, from*). The phrases we can't see are called *functional phrases*, because their heads are functional items we can't see. These heads include tense, agreement, and what we call *complementizer* (head of the clause). As such, there are tense phrases, agreement phrases, and complementizer phrases (we'll get concrete in a minute, and even more so, in our example from French later). If we did a bare-bones sketch of the minimal elements of a sentence, it would look like this (you can ignore "Spec," which stands for *Specifier*, a technical term or feature in sentence formation that is tangential to the present discussion):

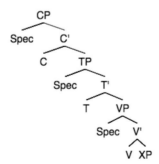

To recap, each phrase gets its name from what is called a *head*. In a noun phrase, the head is a noun. In a verb phrase, the head is a verb. In a tense phrase, the head is an abstract feature called tense (e.g., *eats* vs. *to eat*). In a complementizer phrase, the head is an abstract feature called a complementizer (where words such as *that, which, who, whether,* and the helping verb *do* in *yes/no* questions wind up).

In addition, a phrase's head can be, or is accompanied by, what linguists have called *complements*. In the English verb phrase "drink coffee," "drink" is the head, and "coffee" is the complement. In the English prepositional phrase "at Starbucks," "at" is the head and "Starbucks" is the complement. In the question "Do I drink coffee at Starbucks?" "do" is the head of the complementizer phrase, and the tense phrase (and what's embedded in it) is the complement. Do you see something here? English phrase structure is always *head + complement*. This is why English word order looks the way it does: [do + I drink coffee at Starbucks], [drink + coffee] [at + Starbucks], and so on.

Linguists call English a *head-initial language*. Spanish, French, and Chinese are other head-initial languages; the head is in initial position and precedes the complement in phrase structure.

Now, what about Japanese? Japanese has the opposite phrase structure of English. Japanese is *complement + head*. This is why we get the word order in Japanese that we do: [*Watashi ga sutaabakkusu de kohii o nomimasu + ka*], [*kohii o + nomimasu*] , [*sutsabakkusu + de*], and on down the line of phrases. Japanese, like Turkish, Korean, Classical Latin and many other languages, is what linguists call a *head-final language*. The heads of phrases are always in final position and follow the complement.

> The abstract notions of phrase structure and what is called "head directionality" underlie all language word order.

What's the point? This abstract notion of languages—phrase structure and "head directionality"—underlies all basic word order in languages. The learner of Japanese is taught different "rules": "The verb goes at the end of the sentence," "The question particle goes at the end of a sentence to make a *yes/no* question," "Japanese doesn't have prepositions, it has postpositions, so put them after the noun," among others. But what winds up in the learner's head is not these "rules" but the nature of phrase structure and that Japanese is head-final. In other words, in the learner's unconscious internal system is something like this (where XP stands for any kind of phrase): XP = X + complement (for English) or XP = complement + X (for Japanese). This is our first example that the "rules" given to learners have no psychological validity because what must be acquired is something quite different and much more abstract. Furthermore, the mind/brain is equipped to deal with phrase structure and directionality, so these things don't even need to be taught. Phrase structure is built into the architecture of how languages work, and every unimpaired human mind can put this abstraction representation to work in language acquisition.

Before you go on...

Megan Smith and I have researched the acquisition of phrase structure and head directionality in Japanese, examining learners who knew absolutely no Japanese and no other language like it. We found that, for some learners, underlying representation for phrase structure order is acquired rather quickly, after initial exposure to just 100 sentences. Other learners might take a bit longer, but not that much longer. What was interesting in this study was that the learners could project phrase structure to phrases they hadn't encountered! In our study, they encountered only verb-phrases and postposition-phrases, but we surprise-tested them on other phrases. In short, they were demonstrating "intuitions" about Japanese structure the had not encountered after only 100 sentences. In your own language learning, have you encountered this phenomenon? That is, did you realize that you "knew" something but don't really know what you knew or how you came to know it? (The study is listed in the readings section at the end of this chapter.)

An Example from French

Our second example is something all beginning and intermediate students of French learn. In French, past participles (e.g., "I have *driven*," "I have *dived*," "I have *eaten*," "I have *made*") are marked for agreement under certain conditions. This is what students learn and practice. (By the way, the extra 'e' on the participle is how French indicates feminine agreement in writing. An 's' would be added if plurality were involved. Due to the particulars of French, sometimes you can't hear the difference between masculine and feminine or singular and plural in spoken French, and other times you can.)

- Past participles agree with the subject in the *passé composé* when the verb is être. Example: *Marie a etudié* ("Mary studied") but *Marie est arrivée* ("Mary arrived")

- Past participles agree with subjects when the verb is pronominal (reflexive). Example: *Marie a levé la main* ("Mary raised her hand") but *Marie s'est levée* ("Mary got up," lit: "raised herself up")

- Past participles agree with subjects in passive structures. Example: *Le policier a arrêté Marie* ("The policeman arrested Mary") but *Marie a été arrêtée* ("Marie was arrested")

- Past participles agree with a direct object pronoun. Example: *Le policier a arrêté Marie* ("The policeman arrested Mary") but *Le policier l'a arrêtée* ("The policeman arrested her.")

So what students learn are four distinct "rules" for the application of agreement with past participles. For many teachers and students, these rules seem real. After all, we can see the agreement, right? And these rules are in textbooks, right? But what if all four "rules" were surface manifestations of something deeper and more abstract? Before we go on, let's remind ourselves of the skeletal structure of a head-initial language such as French:

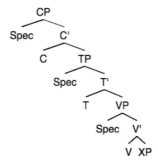

For this discussion, we will shorthand this tree structure the way linguists do. We will use brackets to indicate the stacking of phrases upon phrases, or the nestling of phrases within phrases. Our skeletal structure would then look like this (with certain parts of the tree removed for convenience and simplification):

$$[_{CP} [_C] [_{TP} [_T] [_{VP} [_v] [_{XP}]]]]$$

If your head is spinning from this abstract notation of the basic structure of a sentence, this might be a good time to take a "brain break" and return to the tree and brackets in a few minutes. I remember when I first studied linguistics, I had to learn a whole new way to talk about language. And here we're focusing on only the most basic elements of syntax. (As we begin to stick words inside the brackets, I hope it will be easier to visualize.)

Now that we have basic sentence structure in mind, we can talk about the four rules for agreement of French past participles. Let's start with the nature of verbs. In language, verbs are not all alike, and one way they differ is according to whether the subject of a sentence originates outside or within the verb. For example, for a verb like *eat*, the subject originates outside the verb. In linguistics we would say it looks like:

$$[_{TP} a [_{VP} \text{Marie} [_v \text{mangé}]]]$$

Note that the subject is not inside the bracket with the v that indicates where the verb is, so the subject is not part of the verb. Because of the way language works— and French in particular—the final sentence we actually hear or see has this underlying structure:

$$[_{TP} \text{Marie a} [_{VP} \text{--} [_v \text{mangé}]]]$$

The dashes indicate that *Marie* had to move out of its spot to fulfill certain sentence requirements because of the nature of sentential subjects. What are those requirements? Let's forget about them for now—and for those syntacticians out there, sorry for the shortcuts—I want to keep things as simple as possible.

A verb like *arrive*, on the other hand, has a subject that originates "inside" the verb. So in linguistics we would say the sentence starts out like this (NP = noun phrase):

$$[_{TP} \text{est} [_{VP} [_v \text{arrivé} [_{NP} \text{Marie}]]]]$$

The noun *Marie* is inside the v bracket; that is, the noun phrase containing

Marie is nestled inside the v bracket, so the subject originates inside the verb. What we actually hear or see in the final version of the sentence has an underlying structure like:

$$[_{TP} \text{ Marie est } [_{VP} \text{ -- } [_v \text{ arrivée } [_{NP} \text{ --}]]]]$$

Once again the dashes indicate that *Marie* had to move out of its spot to fulfill sentence requirements. Because I know you're dying of curiosity, here's why *Marie* moved. Sentences require something to—at some point—land in the tense phrase to be the sentence's subject. Of course, not just anything can be the subject, but whatever is allowed as a subject winds up in a particular spot inside the tense phrase, otherwise the sentence has no subject.

> Verbs are not all alike. They differ as to whether the subject of the sentence originates within the verb or not. Wow!

Before you go on...

You might be thinking, "How can a subject originate inside or outside the verb?" Here's one example (of many) to show you why linguists have determined there must be different places in which subjects originate. Let's look at this sentence: *The captain sank the boat.* Here *the captain* is the subject and *the boat* is the object. As the object, *the boat* originates inside the verb as in $[_{TP}$ The captain $[_{VP}$ -- $[_v$ sank $[_{NP}$ the boat]]]]. This sentence answers the question "What did the captain do?" Now consider the question "What happened to the boat?" The answer is: *The boat sank.* Now the boat is the subject: $[_{TP}$ the boat $[_{VP}$ $[_v$ sank $[_{NP}$ --]]]]. We know that, in actuality, something sank the boat or caused it to sink but that entity is not expressed. But the sentence must have a subject. So *boat* is moved out of its object position and "promoted" to subject. Here we see how two different yet related sentences have subjects that come from two different relationships to the verb. See if you can do the same with the verb *break/broke* or the verb *melt/melted*: show how an object can become the subject.

In our French sentences so far, what's the difference between the sentence that has agreement with the past participle and the one that doesn't? In the one that has agreement, something moved out of the v bracket to appear higher up in the sentence. Hmmm.

Now let's look at the sentences with and without object pronouns. Here's the sentence without an object pronoun:

$$[_{TP} \, a \, [_{VP} \, le \, policier \, [_V \, arrêté \, [_{NP} \, Marie]]]]$$

The sentence becomes $[_{TP} \, le \, policier \, a \, [_{VP} \, -\text{-}[_V \, arrêté \, [_{NP} \, Marie]]]]$. Now here's the sentence with an object pronoun:

$$[_{TP} \, a \, [_{VP} \, le \, policier \, [_V \, arrêté \, [_{NP} \, la]]]]$$

It becomes $[_{TP} \, le \, policier \, l'a \, [_{VP} \, -\text{-} \, [_V \, arrêtée \, [_{NP} \, -\text{-}]]]]$. What do we see here? Once again, agreement happens when something moves out from inside the v and appears higher up in the sentence. In this case, the object pronoun moved out from inside the verb and up into the tense phrase.

Let's look at one more example. Here we'll contrast reflexive and non-reflexive verbs. We'll start with the non-reflexive:

$$[_{TP} \, a \, [_{VP} \, Marie \, [_V \, levé \, [_{NP} \, la \, main]]]]$$

This version becomes $[_{TP} \, Marie \, a \, [_{VP} \, -\text{-} \, [_V \, levé \, [_{NP} \, la \, main]]]]$. Now here's what happens to the reflexive sentence:

$$[_{TP} \, est \, [_{VP} \, Marie \, [_V \, levé \, [_{NP} \, se]]]]$$

As you may have guessed, the sentence becomes $[_{TP} \, Marie \, s'est \, [_{VP} \, -\text{-} \, [_V \, levée \, [_{NP} \, -\text{-}]]]]$.

See what's going on here? Once again, like in the previous examples, something moved out from inside the verb and climbed over it to a higher position in the sentence, and now we have agreement. We could illustrate with the passive as well, but you can probably work it out in your head. After all, the object becomes the subject when you go from active to passive; kind of like—but not the exactly same as—the *boat/sink* example in the **Before you go on** box above.

You may have noticed that I have repeatedly said something has moved out from inside the v to higher up into the sentence. What does "higher up" mean? After all, we were looking at sentences as though they had left-to-right word order. But remember that the use of brackets is a shorthand way not to take up page space represented by syntactic trees. So now let's take one sentence and display it in terms of how linguists actually think about language. Let's use the sentence with an object pronoun. We'll take the bracketed notations and display them as trees (except that I'm cutting corners again for simplicity sake). Here's how the sentence starts (and we're leaving out the CP again to keep things simple):

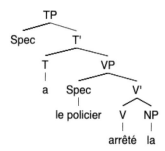

Now, here's what happens to that sentence when the things we're talking about move.

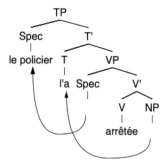

As you can see, the direct object pronoun moves out from inside the verb and higher up into the tense phrase. It is this movement out of the verb and higher up that triggers agreement on past participles.

So what does this all mean? It means that we have one very abstract set of notions about language—where nouns and noun phrases originate as subjects and objects, what classes of verbs there are, movement of things in a sentence, among others, all grounded in other abstract notions we haven't even touched on here—that unify four different "rules" into one single phenomenon: *When something moves out from inside the verb into a higher position in the sentence in French, agreement is triggered.* What winds up in someone's head—whether a native speaker or a non-native speaker—is this abstract information. The learner doesn't acquire four different rules. Over the course of the time, the learner acquires how things move in French and the consequences of movement. So the four textbook rules are external descriptions of something much more abstract and uniform at a deep level. As such, the textbook rules aren't psychologically real, because they don't wind up in someone's mental representation. They're like constellations: they're what we *think* we see, but in reality something much different exists.

Before you go on...

You might think this movement stuff is all hooey. How do we know things move? Just look at the simple case of questions that use *wh-* words like *why, when, where, how,* and so on. There are two versions of each: *What do you study?* and *You study what?* Clearly these sentences are related and mean the same thing. But in one, the *wh-* word has left its spot as the object of the verb and moved higher up and above an inserted helping verb, *do.* And consider the *boat/sink* example where the object moved out of its spot to become the subject. Hidden movement in sentences is well motivated in linguistic theory. It's one of the most basic syntactic operations, and although languages may differ on what is moved and the consequences of that movement, all languages have some kind of movement. And guess what—the learner's mind/brain comes equipped to deal with this. Is this a novel way of looking at language and language acquisition for you? Or is this something you've already learned about, read about, or had discussions on?

Okay. We just reviewed a really hard example. Thinking about sentences as stacks of phrases with movement and consequences of movement is just not what most of us are used to thinking about. I hope the final example will be less complicated but still demonstrative of the abstract nature of language. The example comes from Spanish, so, Spanish teachers, get ready.

An Example from Spanish

If you teach Spanish, you've probably seen textbooks that state that some verbs "change meaning" in the past tense. As I was writing this chapter,

I did a Google search for this topic and found various sites and videos to teach this concept to students. Here are three common examples we can find in textbooks and online sites.

- *conocer*: "to know someone," as in: *Conozco a Charlie. Es un buen amigo.* ("I know Charlie. He's a good friend.") But in the past tense (preterit) it means "to meet," as in *Anoche conocí a una persona fabulosa.* ("Last night I met a fabulous person.")

- *saber*: "to know something," as in: *Sé que Charlie está en su primer año.* ("I know Charlie is a freshman.") But in the past tense (preterit) it means "to find out," as in: *Anoche supe que Charlie está en su primer año.* ("Last night I found out Charlie was a freshman.")

- *querer*: "to want," as in *Quiero ser presidente.* ("I want to be president.") But in the past tense (preterit) it means "tried to," as in *Quise ser presidente.* ("I tried to be president.") And in the negative it means "refused to" as in *No quise ser presidente.* ("I refused to be president.")

However, verbs don't change meaning in languages from tense to tense. In Spanish, the three verbs sampled here don't change meaning. To the Spanish speaker they always mean what they

> Verbs don't change meaning from tense to tense.

mean. The problem is that English doesn't encode aspectual information the way Spanish does and, in some cases, must rely on different words to convey a meaning that in Spanish is encoded grammatically. What do I mean by "aspectual information"?

All events have what linguists call *aspect*, which refers to how the event is viewed in the speaker's mind as the speaker reports it. That event could have a beginning or end point (either point is called a "boundary") or not. For example, when I talk about knowing someone, I do not refer to when I began to know that person or when I might stop knowing that person. But when I talk in the past, I can explicitly or implicitly refer to a beginning or end point of that knowing. English does this lexically (i.e., by using a different word): "I already *knew* Charlie before the party" vs. "I *met* Charlie at the party" (*met* = "I began to know him"). Spanish does this with the difference between preterit and imperfect verb endings: *Ya conocía a Charlie antes de la fiesta* vs. *Conocí a Charlie en la fiesta*. So what I am actually indicating with the verb form *conocí* is that I began to know Charlie. I'm indicating a boundary to the event of knowing; in this case, the beginning. The verb didn't change meaning.

Likewise with the verb *querer* ("want") in Spanish. It does not mean "tried to" when used with the preterit tense. It still means "want." But what I signal when I say *Quise ser presidente* is that my desire ended at some point (or in some cases, the desire began at a particular point in time). I indicate to the listener that I'm putting a boundary on the event; in this case, the end point. The same is true for its use in a negative sentence. When I say *No quise ser presidente*, I'm indicating I didn't want to be president and am putting a boundary on that wanting (in this case, that my not wanting to be president started at a particular point in time).

When we indicate boundaries on events, we refer to what linguists call *perfectivity*. A perfective event has a boundary. A non-perfective event doesn't. Languages like Spanish have grammatical devices to indicate perfectivity. These devices interact with different classes of events to express different kinds of meaning. *Aspect* and *perfectivity* are rather abstract concepts and largely unteachable to language students—just ask any Spanish or French teacher who has struggled with this concept. I've observed enough Spanish and French teachers over the years to see how some have done everything but stand on their heads to try to convey the differences indicated by the preterit/*passé composé* and the imperfect/*imparfait* in the past tense. The good news is that, as learners progress in their interaction with Spanish (and French) and interact more and more with narratives using past tenses, they develop the underlying representation for perfectivity and how it works in Spanish (though it takes some time). The mind/brain is equipped to do this. As we keep saying, the rule that "certain verbs change meaning in the past" is not psychologically real. This is not what exists in anyone's head.

By the way, research suggests that teaching students that "verbs change meaning" can actually impede the acquisition of how aspect works. In a 2008 study, Jason Rothman compared classroom and non-classroom learners' knowledge and ability with such verbs as *querer, conocer, saber,* and others and found that those who had classroom study and learned that the verbs changed meaning in the past performed worse than those who did not have the same classroom experience. (I've included this study in the suggested readings if you want to venture into the nitty-gritty of the research yourself.)

Before you go on...

There is a good deal of L2 research on how tense and aspectual systems develop in learners over time. Most of it has been conducted on English and Spanish as second languages. Although learners can and do eventually work out the intricacies of how tense-aspect systems work in a language, this process can take a long time — and, like many things in acquisition, it has developmental stages independent of instruction and correction. On the ACTFL scale, we don't see significant control of tense-aspect until the Advanced level and even then it's not perfect. Most learners don't exhibit native-like ability until a much higher-level proficiency. For example, children learning English as a first language don't get tense marking completely under control until about age five, and they don't have control over passives (e.g., "The dog was chased by the cat") until well into elementary school. Some things just take a long time, right?

A Note on Paradigms

Now you can relax. You've been through all the tough examples of how language is abstract and how what looks like "rules" from the outside isn't what winds up in anyone's head. We could give lots and lots of examples, but this is a short book that is merely illustrative, not exhaustive. In this section, we'll step away from abstract concepts and talk about something else: paradigms.

From Chapter 1 you might remember that paradigms are what teachers call verb charts, charts that summarize case endings, or charts that show how definite articles vary depending on such things as number and gender. We will focus on verb charts here and use Spanish person-number endings. Here's the paradigm from Chapter 1.

	SINGULAR	PLURAL
1ST	-o/ -oy	-mos
2ND	-s	-is
3RD	-a/-e	-n

Spanish has what is called "rich person-number morphology," a fancy way to say that it has different verb endings, depending on who or what the verb refers to. Textbooks unfailingly present this paradigm, and many teachers dutifully teach it and lead their students in practice of it, hoping they will "master the endings." Everyone thinks this is what winds up in our heads—and when you think about it, there's nothing really abstract about the difference, say, between you (second-person singular) and me (first-person singular).

But paradigms aren't what wind up in people's heads. The research suggests that verbs are encoded into your mental dictionary as whole things—endings

> Paradigms aren't what wind up in people's heads.

and all. In Spanish, for example, the speaker has no infinitive with endings listed somewhere that are combined with the root of the infinitive (i.e., the Spanish textbook rule of "drop the –r and add the appropriate ending" isn't a real rule). Instead, a person first encodes a verb like *estudio* ("I study") as a whole word. That word builds up strength as a person hears and sees it in communicative contexts again and again. Another verb such as *vivo* ("I live") is also encoded as a whole word. Because the two words share an underlying meaning (first-person singular) they are connected in the mental dictionary. Imagine something like this:

Now let's imagine that the mental dictionary is building up and someone hears and sees the word *tengo* ("I have") in communicative contexts over and over. This word is encoded and entered into the dictionary. Because it shares the underlying meaning of first-person singular, it is connected to the other verbs in this network.

Then another word such as *tomo* ("I drink/take") makes it into the system. It, too, is connected to the others via its shared meaning of first-person singular.

Now, imagine this person hears more and more verbs such as these—hundreds or lots of hundreds. What winds up is a vast interconnected network of words, all sharing the same underlying meaning of first-person singular. When a person hears *vivo* in context, that person does not access *viv-* as a root and the ending *–o* somewhere. Instead, the person accesses the entire word *vivo* from the mental dictionary to understand what the other person is saying. Likewise, when this person speaks, that person is not generating *viv-* and adding an *–o* but is pulling down *vivo* from his network and using the whole word. For the record, the verbs would also be connected to other forms that share the root, so *vivo* would be connected to *viví* ("I lived"), *viven* ("they live"), and even *vivienda* ("dwelling/place where one lives"), while *estudio* would be connected to other items such as *estudiante* ("student") and *estudioso* ("studious").

So what happens when a person with this network encounters a new word in the input (communicative context) such as *entiendo* ("I understand")? Assuming the person can deduce the meaning from context, i.e., that the person is talking about understanding something, the other verbs in the system that end in *–o* are activated because of the similar sound they share. (They also share other properties, but we'll get to that in a minute.) This is how the person is able to understand and "compute" new words: by activation of other words that share something with that word.

What all of this means is that no one walks around with infinitives or roots for verbs in their heads to which they attach person-number endings. People don't have a rule in their heads such as "drop the *–ar* or *–er/–ir* ending and add an *–o*," for example. Instead these endings are "derived in the moment" as needed from the thousands of stored whole words. And this is true for not just verb endings but also noun endings, articles, and other things. To be sure, for easy access during language use, stored words must be robustly represented enough so comprehension and speaking aren't slowed down too much. This is why we see slow-downs in what is called "reaction time research" when words are less frequent and less familiar to native and non-native speakers. Researchers have consistently shown that very high-frequency words are retrieved and used much more quickly in laboratory studies than low-frequency words when matched for sounds, length, endings, prefixes, and all other possible variables.

At first blush, this mental dictionary is not a very abstract system. Words are tagged with meaning, enter the mental dictionary, and endings are "derived" as needed. Simple, right? So here's the somewhat (but not too) abstract part. You're probably used to thinking of words as bits of meaning—and you're right. But they have hidden and abstract features attached to them.

Let's take the simple word *tengo* ("I have") to show what is embedded inside this word in the mental dictionary. First, its meaning has something to do with possession, the details of which are abstract in and of themselves. Then it is tagged as a verb, not a noun, with these features: [-N, +V]. Of course, the definitions of 'noun' and 'verb,' take us into a whole other realm of abstraction. No, nouns and verbs are not what teachers are used to telling their students in class or what students learned in grade-school "grammar" courses. They're much more abstract entities that are difficult to define in everyday terms.

The word *tengo* must also be tagged for present tense, not past tense, so embedded within it are these features: [+ present, – past]. It is tagged, of course, for person and number: [1st] [-plural]. It must eventually be tagged for its verb class (Spanish has three classes: –a, –e, and –i class verbs). So somewhere it has this feature: [e]. On top of all of this, it must be encoded phonologically, according to the sounds themselves. And there is more to this word than what we are listing here; when *tengo* is robustly represented in your head as a Spanish speaker, it has an entry something like this:

ˈtɛ̃ŋ.go [this is how the sounds are represented]
[meaning: something about possession]
[-N, +V]
[e class verb]
[+present, -past]

[1st]

[-plural]

[and anything else we've forgotten here]

What this romp through the verb *tengo* shows is just how much hidden stuff goes into the encoding of one little everyday word. When you think about it, it's pretty amazing, especially if you consider everything else going on in a sentence. But that's the subject of the next chapter.

Before you go on...

We just examined the verb *tengo* in Spanish. Have you ever asked yourself what a verb is? If you do an Internet search, you'd find something like this (from Merriam-Webster): *a word that characteristically is the grammatical center of a predicate and expresses an act, occurrence, or mode of being, that in various languages is inflected for agreement with the subject, for tense, for voice, for mood, or for aspect, and that typically has rather full descriptive meaning and characterizing quality but is sometimes nearly devoid of these especially when used as an auxiliary or linking verb.* Can you see how this definition tries to be complete but is inadequate, if not inaccurate? What's more, look at all the undefined constructs within this definition: *predicate, agreement, tense, voice, mood, aspect, descriptive meaning, quality, auxiliary.* There's a lot of hidden abstraction, even in this limited definition! Once again you go down a rabbit hole trying to define something as ubiquitous as 'verb.' Try asking friends and family members to define what a verb is. What do they come up with? Can you determine the origins of their responses (e.g., something they learned in English class, something they're making up because you asked them to think about it, something they read somewhere)?

Some Final Comments

In this chapter we have seen three instances of "rules" from different languages that are found in textbooks and online sources. The point is that these so-called rules aren't really rules at all but external descriptions of something much deeper and more abstract that defies easy explanation—unless you want to study linguistics. We also touched on how paradigms aren't psychologically real either; that no one walks around with "charts" in their heads or rules to convert an infinitive into an inflected verb. (By the way, an infinitive is an inflected verb in languages like Spanish and French. It's just not inflected for tense or anything else.) Like rules, paradigms and charts are an external description of things that look much different on the inside of someone's head.

This is supposed to be a brief book—something to get you on the road to thinking about language differently, if you haven't already done that. To that end, we reviewed only a few examples, but at least we looked at a number of different types of things from different languages. So that counts for something. No matter: textbooks and websites are full of "rules," "patterns," "paradigms," and the like. Most if not all are simply not real, psychologically speaking. Yet teachers and students rely on them and think they are. Students (and teachers) think the rules are what they're "internalizing."

I won't speculate why people think this (although I have ideas about that). I will end this chapter by saying that, until the language teaching profession deals with the abstract nature of language, we will forever be engaged in discussions about whether this or that method/technique works for language teaching because we have failed to grapple with the essence of language. And we argue with each other because the very basic nature of what we are talking about escapes us. Our arguments are based on our perceptions of the surface of language embodied in "rules," "patterns," "paradigms," and the like. We are teaching constellations rather than understanding how the universe works.

References and Suggested Readings

Burton, S., Dechaine, R., & Vatikiotis-Bateson, E. (2012). *Linguistics for dummies*. Mississaugua, Ontario: John Wiley & Sons. (I wouldn't normally recommend a book like this, but this might be a good one to read before you venture into a hardcore linguistics text.)

Carnie, A. (2012). *Syntax: a generative introduction* (3rd edition). Oxford: Blackwell. (This is only for those who want to take a heavy-duty course!)
Pinker, S. (2007). *The language instinct.* (See especially Chapter 4 on how language works.) New York: Harper Perennial.

Rothman, J. (2008). Aspect selection in adult L2 Spanish and the Competing Systems hypothesis: When pedagogical and linguistic rules conflict. *Languages in Contrast, 8*, 74-106.

VanPatten, B., & Smith, M. (2015). Aptitude as grammatical sensitivity and the initial stages of learning Japanese as an L2: Parametric variation and case marking. *Studies in Second-language acquisition, 37*, 135-165.

Think About It

1. We started this chapter with a question: Which concept would you label as concrete and which as abstract: *email message* and *round*? List at least five other concepts we use in our daily lives that are abstract and almost impossible to define without going down a rabbit hole.

2. A comment we often hear is: "Rules have exceptions." Linguists might argue, however, that languages don't like exceptions and are highly regular. What do you think of this statement, in light of what you've read in this chapter? Here's one thing you might think about: phrase structure in Japanese and English are what you read about head-final and head-initial phrases.

3. Several times in this chapter and in the question above, we have distinguished between a description and a rule. For example, textbook rules are an attempt to describe something internal but fail in their descriptions. What's the difference between a rule and a description?

4. The focus of this chapter is the abstract nature of language. Have you asked yourself what 'abstract' means? Conduct an Internet search on the meaning of this word. How do these definitions fit within the ideas in this chapter? In what ways don't they? Can you define 'abstract'?

5. In one of the ***Before you go on…*** boxes, we touched on the nature of verbs—that is, what is a verb? As you consider your definition, keep the following in mind:

   - The following are all verbs: *eat, run, arrive, blink, think, realize, seem, die, rain, seem, disappear,* and *be.*

   - Chinese has no endings on verbs (for anything!), and English has third-person singular in the present tense (no other person-number markings anywhere) and inflects verbs for pastness (e.g., 'watched') and imperfectivity (e.g., 'watching') only. It uses modals for other things (e.g., *will, would, might*).

- Some languages allow verbless sentences (e.g., Chinese and Arabic can both say 'John tall' for 'John is tall').

6. Given what you've read so far, it is easy to conclude that teaching and learning textbook rules is a waste of time if they do not ultimately wind up in someone's head. And this would be a valid conclusion. But are there other reasons for studying and learning textbook rules unrelated to this conclusion?

7. If you were to convert the main idea(s) of this chapter into a short talking point, what would that be? How could you use that talking point to initiate a conversation with parents, administrators, colleagues, and others? If you engaged in conversation, what kind of example could you give to other people?

Chapter 3

Language is Complex

3

At the beginning of the previous chapter, we looked at the concept *round* and determined it was much more abstract than what meets the eye. It is abstract because it is almost impossible to define in everyday language—that is, if we want to actually capture what roundness is. We could resort to a technical definition like this: "The properties of an object or design whose surface or linear points are all equidistant from a center." Got it? Now define these constructs: *properties, surface, linear, points, equidistant,* and *center.* Hmmm. Not so easy to unpack and define *round*, is it?

The point of this example is that the concept of *round* is complex as well as abstract. Various other abstract concepts come to bear on its definition so that abstraction is layered upon abstraction and construct intersects with construct. In this chapter, we will take language another step and show how it is both abstract and complex. At every level of even the simplest sentence, multiple constructs come into play. It can be mind-boggling.

To help us see this complexity, let's explore this sentence: "Murphy's not leaving." It's a super-simple sentence at first glance. To see that there's much more than meets the eye, let's start with meaning.

Meaning

Imagine someone walking up to you or calling you on the phone and beginning the conversation with "Murphy's not leaving." Though this sentence comes out of the blue (i.e., it's the first thing out of this person's mouth), you are expected to grasp its meaning and intent. Let's start with intent. You know that this sentence is a declarative and not a question when you hear it, right? But could it be a question? Could it be something else? What is the intent of the speaker? Depending on tone, intonation, and other aspects of how the person actually says the sentence, there are at least four possibilities, each illustrated with appropriate responses. Try to sound out how the sentences might be spoken to indicate different intent each time.

- It is an announcement. The person is letting you know about a situation, which is that Murphy is not leaving.

    A: Murphy's not leaving.
    B: I know. I just found out.

- It is a complaint. The person is letting you know that Murphy's not leaving, as well as how he feels about the situation. He's not happy.

    A: Murphy's not leaving.
    B: I don't like it either.

- It is a question. The person is guessing the situation is true and wants you to confirm it with a 'yes' or 'no.'

    A: Murphy's not leaving?
    B: No. He's not.

- It is a surprise. The person uttering this sentence is letting you know he did not know this fact.

    A: Murphy's not leaving.
    B: I know, right? I was surprised, too.

What we see in these different possibilities is that what a sentence means partly depends on how it is spoken. With a certain intonational contour, it is an announcement. With another, it is a complaint. With yet another, it could be something else. Right off the bat we see that we already have an intertwining of sentential meaning and what we call *prosody*. Prosody refers, in part, to the stress, pitch, rhythm, and otherwise "tone" of a sentence. For example, typical questions such as "Is Murphy leaving?" have a different intonational contour from simple statements such as "I need to buy milk." Languages differ in their intonational contours, but speakers use them to indicate intent or purpose of an utterance. Some linguists would even argue that prosody is as important

> Both prosody and assumed or real world knowledge come into play in the meaning of a sentence.

to sentence comprehension as knowing words and the relationships between them. (By the way, the branch of linguistics that deals with speaker intent at the sentence level is called *pragmatics*.)

Okay. So already we see a level of complexity in a simple sentence. With this example is another level of meaning: what the speaker believes you know and can infer about what is being said. First, the speaker assumes you know who Murphy is. It would be pretty weird for someone to say this to you without that assumption. Second, the speaker also assumes you know there is some history here—that there were rumors Murphy was moving out of state, that he was fired, that he had an offer from someone else. Every time someone utters a sentence directed at someone else (same for signing!), the speaker makes assumptions about what the person knows and doesn't know.

This, then, adds another level of complexity to sentence meaning: real word knowledge and shared knowledge. So far, then, we see that, for the meaning of a sentence, both speaker intent (prosody) and assumed and/or shared knowledge about the world come into play. But we're not done yet.

Before you go on...

Think back on a possible recent interchange you had with someone in which you misinterpreted or misunderstood what the person said. Did you not pick up on the prosodic cues? Did that person assume you knew something you didn't? How did you "resolve" the misinterpretation/misunderstanding? In such an example, we are in the realm of how language works in communication (i.e., the expression and interpretation of meaning in a given context for a given purpose). So, when language is put to use for communication, it automatically operates beyond the level of what individual words mean or what the sentence structure is.

At the sentence's micro level, the speaker assumes you have a mental dictionary—a lexicon—with certain words in it. For example, the speaker believes you know what the word "leaving" means. And you probably do. Even "leave" or "leaving" is complex with all of the features and embedded meaning in it. For example, "leave" has at least two different meanings in English: (1) effecting a departure, and (2) not taking something with someone (e.g., "Murphy's not leaving the firm" vs. "Murphy's not leaving the book for you"). You have to decide which meaning of "leave" is intended when you hear "Murphy's not leaving." Syntax and its interface with semantics helps you with that, which we will see in a minute. In short, even the simplest of sentences can be complex in the sense of the multiple layers of meaning involved—and we're just scratching the surface.

Syntax and Morphology (and some Phonology)

Syntax refers to sentence structure. This structure is determined by constraints that lurk behind the sentence. We saw examples of this in the previous chapter. When most teachers think of sentence structure, they think of textbook rules. For example, the English teacher might say, "Use the auxiliary 'be' with a verb ending in –*ing* to form the progressive." But in our simple little sentence lurks some hidden syntactic "stuff" you probably haven't thought about. Let's start with the verb "leave."

As we mentioned above, at least two different versions of the verb "leave" are in your head; you have two different lexical entries in your mental dictionary. One lexical entry refers to departure, the other to not taking something with someone. In your mental dictionary, these verbs have some distinct features. Here we will look at only a couple of the relevant ones for this discussion.

leave$_1$: [meaning: not take something], [-N, +V], [agent, patient, optional: recipient with 'for']

leave$_2$: [meaning: depart], [-N, +V], [theme, optional: locative]

In the first "leave," note, that the lexical entry says the verb has minimally two entities that are part of the verb's underlying meaning: an agent and a patient. The agent performs the action of leaving, and the patient is the thing left. So, in the sentence "Murphy is leaving the book," Murphy is the agent, and the book is the patient. There is also an optional third entity, so we can sometimes get sentences like "Murphy's not leaving the book for you." However, with the second lexical entry, the underlying meaning of the verb has only a theme. Different from a patient, a theme is defined by linguists as something that undergoes location or relocation. Verbs like *arrive, leave, come, go, fall, jump,* and others have only themes, not agents. By the way, agents, patients, themes, and similar linguistic constructs are the underlying "roles" or "arguments" of the verb. We'll use the word "roles" to keep it simple.

(Linguists are not entirely in agreement about the difference between themes and patients, but that's not important here.)

So what does this all mean for this little sentence? Underlying verbal roles such as agents, patients, and themes must be expressed in the sentence if the verb requires them. That is, the syntax demands representation of required roles somewhere in the sentence. If they are optional, they are expressed only if they are relevant to the meaning at hand. Note that the first "leave" above requires an agent and a patient, while the second "leave" requires only a theme. This is what helps the listener know which meaning you intend. When the listener hears "Murphy's not leaving" and nothing follows "leaving," the listener's internal devices determine that the speaker means the second "leave" and that Murphy is the theme of "leaving." Otherwise, more nouns or noun phrases would appear in the sentence to express the roles embedded in the verb. When the listener hears "Murphy's leaving a book for you," that person knows you intend the other meaning of "leave," because now three entities are expressed in the sentence. With this example, then, we see interplay between syntax and underlying meaning, another level of complexity. This underlying meaning of verbs and their roles is part of what we call *semantics*.

> Another level of complexity is found in the interplay between syntax and underlying meaning, or semantics.

Before you go on...

Verbs vary as to the number of underlying roles they have and what they represent. Some verbs only have one required role as in *die*: "My turtle died." In this case, *die* requires an experiencer and only an experiencer. Some verbs require one role with an optional other role as in *eat*: "John is eating" and "John is eating an apple"—in this case, an agent and an optional patient. Other verbs require two roles as in *hit*: "John hit the ball." We can't say simply *"John hit." Our natural response is to say, "He hit *what*? Finish the sentence, will you?" Some verbs require three underlying roles such as *put*: "Murphy put the cake in the oven." Any version of this sentence without three entities involved (agent, theme, destination) would be ungrammatical. So the underlying meaning of verbs strongly affects basic sentence structure. How does this discussion link to what you have learned about transitive and intransitive verbs? Did you know that, for example, *die* and *arrive* are intransitive, but for different reasons?

Remember our example from French in Chapter 2—the example about agreement with past participles? What we saw is that people wind up with a linguistic system in French that says that anytime something moves out from inside the verb and crosses over and higher up into the syntax of the sentence, agreement is triggered. With English "leave" the theme originates inside the verb: [$_{TP}$ [$_{NEGP}$ not [$_{VP}$ [$_V$ leaving [$_{NP}$ Murphy]]]]. It must move out and up to the TP to become a subject, or the sentence is not grammatical: [$_{TP}$ Murphy [$_{NEGP}$ not [$_{VP}$ [$_V$ leaving [$_{NP}$ ---]]]]]. Just thought we should be reminded of this little detail, as it adds to the complexity.

Because "leave" is a verb, it can appear in different forms: *leave, leaves, left, leaving*. These different forms result from the *morphology* of words, a fancy way of saying the "word's shape." The shape of a word involves its root (which carries basic meaning) and inflections (e.g., endings), prefixes, and other "things" attached to the word (e.g, "decorate", "redecorate", "decorating") . Nouns, verbs, determiners (e.g., definite and indefinite articles, possessives like "my" and "his," demonstratives like "this" and "those"), and other categories of words can have different shapes because of the way morphology works in any given language. In our example, the verb is "leaving." Why is it "leaving" and not "leaves," for example? Because hidden within the syntax of the sentence is the meaning "in progress"—or our friend from Chapter 2, perfectivity. In this case, it's non-perfectivity. The speaker who utters this sentence has in mind that the event of "leave" has no boundary. That is, the speaker does not wish or need to indicate a beginning or end of the event. This requires the use of –*ing* in English to indicate this meaning. Any other form of the verb just won't do. In this case, we have an intersection of syntax, morphology, and meaning that causes the insertion of "leaving" into the sentence, not "leaves," "left" or any other possible version of the verb. Still more complexity!

But we're not quite done. English requires something to carry tense features for a sentence to be grammatical. The verb form "leaving" is tenseless. The use of –*ing* is related to perfectivity, not to tense.

Morphology and syntax interact adding more complexity to a sentence.

How do we know? Because the –*ing* can be found in present, past and future sentences: "He was leaving", "He is leaving", "He will be leaving." So the auxiliary "be" is inserted into the tense phrase to meet the requirement that, in English, tense must be reflected in the syntax somewhere. In this case the form is *is*, because also encoded somewhere in the sentence is the feature [+ present, − past]: [$_{TP}$ Murphy [$_{T}$ is [$_{NEGP}$ not [$_{VP}$ [$_{V}$ leaving [$_{NP}$ ---]]]]]]. Now we have one thing in the sentence (or lack of it) triggering something else in another part of the sentence. Morphology and syntax interact, adding more complexity to a sentence.

Before you go on...

Not all languages have a tense feature like English. Spanish and French do, but Mandarin Chinese does not. Clearly, Mandarin expresses time frames, but uses lexical items (e.g., "yesterday" "this morning"), whereas English does it both lexically and morphologically on the verb or with modals and auxiliaries (e.g., "I finished it yesterday," "I will be here tomorrow"). And some languages don't make use of a "be" verb as an auxiliary the way English does. In the early stages of language acquisition, whether child L1 or later L2, learners typically omit "be" verbs. And many pidgins (i.e., a contact language developed by people who don't speak the same language) also don't have a "be" verb, even when both contact languages have such verbs.

So just this little sentence, "Murphy's not leaving", has multiple complexities you probably never even thought of.

One final point: English allows contractions with present tense "be" across adjacent elements when nothing intervenes: "I am" → "I'm," "you are" → "you're," "Murphy is" → "Murphy's" (as long as it's not at the end of the sentence; you can't say *"Murphy's leaving but no one else's"; instead, you must say "no one else is"). So when spoken, the intersection of morphology (the shape of a word) and phonology (the sound system) interact to allow the English speaker to say "Murphy's not leaving" with the requirement that the actual sound of the contracted *'s* is not [s] but [z]. That is, it must sound like: [ˈmɜrfiz]. Notice that if we substitute "Murphy" with the phrase "the cat," the contracted "is" sounds like an [s], not a [z]. In short, there is another level of complexity in how the sound system interacts with the morphology and syntax of the sentence.

Summary (So Far)

Before going on, let's summarize the complexity we see in this one little sentence "Murphy's not leaving." We're not listing anything in any particular order.

- *Semantics.* Verbs have underlying roles such as agent, patient, theme, etc., that are projected into the syntax.

- *Syntax.* Sentence structure has constraints, and may indicate what meaning is intended (e.g., "leave" as intransitive vs. "leave" as transitive).

- *Morphology.* The 'leaving' form of the verb is required because of the intended meaning of no beginning and no end. Once "leaving" is selected, it triggers the need for an auxiliary verb to carry tense.

- *Phonology.* The syntax of English allows for contractions and when "is" is reduced to "-s," it must be [z] as opposed to [s] in this example.

- *Prosody and sentential meaning.* Depending on how the speaker uses pitch, rhythm, and other parts of intonational contour, we will understand the speaker's intent (e.g., a mere statement of fact, a complaint, showing surprise).

- *Assumed or shared knowledge and meaning.* The words chosen and how the speaker utters the sentence depends on what he or she assumes the listener already knows, as either real-world or as shared knowledge between speaker and listener.

This is quite a list of things happening all at once in the itty-bitty sentence "Murphy's not leaving." We could list more, but you're probably exhausted from thinking about just this one sentence. Nonetheless, we will list a few more things in the next section.

Discourse

Sentences don't exist in a vacuum. They are always part of *discourse.* Discourse refers the connection of sentences to make a larger meaning. Let's imagine this short conversation:

Me: Murphy's not leaving.
My sister: I was pretty sure he wouldn't.

Let's contrast this with the following interchange:

Me: Murphy's not leaving.
My sister: I prefer chocolate cake.

The first interchange makes sense; the second one doesn't. How does my sister's preference for chocolate cake relate to Murphy's non-departure? In conversations, monologues, paragraphs—in short, wherever two or more sentences are related to each other—some kind of cohesion must exist. That is, the sentences must work together to make a larger meaning: the *discourse* meaning. Cohesion involves a number of elements. Try this exercise, which is called a *discourse scramble*. The following sentences form a paragraph but are not in their original order. Can you put them in some kind of cohesive order?

Sentences don't exist in a vacuum. They are always part of what we call "discourse"—which adds more complexity.

• At least that's what the boss says.

• But my hunch is that his other offer fell through.

• It turns out he changed his mind about the firm and wants to stay.

• Murphy's not leaving.

I bet you could, and it was probably relatively easy—largely because there are only four sentences, and because this paragraph is uncomplicated. Is this what you came up with? "Murphy's not leaving. It turns out he changed his mind about the firm and wants to stay. At least that's what the boss says. But my hunch is that his other offer fell through."

To do this little exercise in discourse cohesion, you relied on syntax, semantics, morphology, real-world knowledge, and a part of syntax that functions at the discourse level: *antecedence*. (Phonology is involved, too, but only to the extent that you hear the sounds in your head as you read; that is, you subvocalize.) *Antecedence* refers to linking something in one sentence (or clause) with something in another sentence (or clause). For example, you had to link "He" in "He changed his mind" with Murphy in the first sentence, "Murphy's not leaving." You also linked "his" in "his other offer" with Murphy and not "the boss," even though both are possible antecedents (unless the boss is female, but this paragraph doesn't specify the boss's gender). Pronouns are syntactic devices typically used to avoid unnecessary repetition of noun phrases. It would sound odd to say, "Murphy's not leaving. It turns out Murphy changed Murphy's mind about the firm and wants to stay."

So discourse adds another level of complexity when we get into antecedence and how this is expressed in the syntax (e.g., the use of pronouns, possessive determiners) and morphology (e.g., 'he' as opposed to 'she'). For the purpose of this presentation, we are not going to dig more into discourse. The point is to simply show that most sentences don't exist in isolation. They are part of something bigger (discourse) that carries hidden ways in which language works at the sentence level.

Before you go on...

What happens in languages like Spanish and Greek that don't require subject pronouns? In the string "Murphy's not leaving. It turns out he changed his mind." the Spanish version would be: *Murphy no se va. Resulta que cambió de opinión.* In the second sentence we have two "bare" verbs: *resulta* ("it turns out") and *cambió* ("he changed"). A subject pronoun for *resulta* is prohibited in Spanish (i.e., you can't put in an equivalent of "it"), and the subject pronoun is avoided for *cambió* because there is no change in subject or topic from the first sentence. The first is related to syntax; the second is related to discourse involving connections between sentences. Do you see this as another layer of complexity in acquiring a language like Spanish or Greek?

Sentence Computation

Now that we have a working idea of just how complex language is and how abstract it can be, we can marvel at how a speaker of a language, at any level of proficiency beyond the two-word stage, juggles this complexity in real time. If I say, "Murphy's not leaving," you process that sentence in real time, as opposed to thinking about it much later. Real-time language processing is super-fast. The average English speaking rate is 125 to 150 words per minute. This rate suggests that, at the higher end, someone speaks 2.5 words per second. This in turn means that sentence-processing happens in milliseconds. Let's see what this means with the sentence "Murphy's not leaving."

As I hear this sentence, my "processor" kicks into high gear. As soon as I hear "Murphy," my processor begins to make decisions. The processor activates "Murphy" from my mental dictionary with all of its features: [+N, -V] [proper name] [male] [guy I work with], and any other relevant information. As this information is activated, I begin sentence computation and project a noun phrase, NP, and initially determine (unconsciously, of course) that this will be the subject of the sentence: $[_{TP} [_{NP}$ Murphy]... So far, something like 100 milliseconds has passed. I then process the $'s$ and must determine whether it's a possessive or a contracted form of "is." Either is possible. I activate both of these in my mental dictionary with all of their features (e.g., for the contracted form of "is," [-N, +V] [no meaning] [+present, - past], [3rd] [- plural], and so on). So at the millisecond level I hesitate, then go with the contracted form of "is," and project the contraction as the tense carrier and project a T: $[_{TP} [_{NP}$ Murphy] $[_{T}$'s... Then I hear "not" and activate it in my mental

> Real-time language processing is super-fast. Sentence processing happens at the level of milliseconds.

dictionary along with its meaning and features and project a negative phrase, which in turn confirms my previous decision that the $'s$ must be a contracted form of "be." (Had I heard "dog" next, as in "Murphy's dog." I would have had to immediately backtrack and re-project the $'s$ as a possessive into my sentence computation.) So now I have $[_{TP} [_{NP}$ Murphy] $[_{T}$'s $[_{NEGP}$ not]]... Everything so far has happened within less than one second. Next I hear "leaving" and access this from my mental dictionary along with its features (e.g., [refers to departure] [-N, +V], [-perfective]) and finish the computation: $[_{TP} [_{NP}$ Murphy] $[_{T}$'s $[_{NEGP}$ not $[_{VP}$ leaving]]]. Because I perceive this to be the end of the sentence, I stop computation, and my processor does a quick scan to make sure the sentence makes sense. All of this happens in about 1000 milliseconds = 1 second—maybe a tad longer.

Get the picture? Behind the comprehension of even the most simple sentence is lightning-like computation of structure as well as access to the mental dictionary. This process occurs thousands of times a day for any hearing person. And we haven't touched on *sentence production*. Sentence production is not quite the mirror image of comprehension in terms of real-time processing (depending on who you talk to) but is equally complex and fast.

Given its abstractness and complexity, language is truly miraculous when you think about it. Now imagine acquiring this abstractness and complexity. How is it possible? Surely it doesn't arise from the presentation and practice of textbook "patterns" and "rules." After all, preschoolers do this in their first language. Yes, it takes time. But it can't be learned and practiced in the way people have traditionally assumed. Such abstraction, complexity, and sentence computation develop over time as learners are exposed to input in communicative contexts. That is, after all, how the human mind/brain is wired.

Before you go on...

... I bet you've never thought just how complicated the process of comprehending a sentence really is. See if you can finish this sentence in some way based on what you've read and/or already know: *Comprehension of a sentence involves. . .* You can add as much as you deem necessary to flesh out your idea.

A Note About Acquisition

Although this book is about the nature of language, I feel compelled to touch on acquisition here for a minute. As we just saw, sentences must be "computed" in real time to be understood or spoken. The perplexing thing about acquisition is: because it depends on communicative input and is a byproduct of comprehension, how do learners compute sentences with no language to compute with? The answer is relatively straightforward.

First, we can't speak to learners the way we speak to native speakers. The 125-to-150 words-per-minute speed of regular speech just isn't right for beginners or intermediate learners. So we know right away that learner-centered input must be slower and must contain many more pauses—and probably short sentences. In addition, repetition of key elements and phrases helps learners segment the speech stream to unconsciously find the hidden phrases of language. Here's an example from what might happen on the very first day a learner hears English. The teacher is holding up a picture of a 17-year-old boy.

"This is Murphy. Murphy is a boy."

The teacher tapes that picture to the board and holds up one of a girl about the same age.

"This is Janine. Janine is a girl."

The teacher tapes up the second picture alongside the first.

"Okay. So this is Murphy, a boy. This is Janine, a girl."

The teacher points to Murphy.

"Is this Murphy or is this Janine?"
    [classroom shouts saying "Murphy"]
"Is he a boy or a girl?"
    [classroom shouts saying "boy"]
"Right. He's a boy. And Janine is a girl."

This brief example looks all too familiar to those of us who have worked in comprehension-based classrooms for a while—and also those who use mixed approaches. We've all done something like this in one way or another. But what is worth pointing out is how this kind of segmented input with built-in repetitions helps learners begin to find word boundaries in the speech stream and build underlying phrases that are the heart of sentence structure.

To be sure, we don't know if learners at this point are processing 'boy' = the word for boy or 'a boy' = the word for 'boy' or even 'a boy' = determiner + the word for 'boy.' We know they are isolating something. But with continued examples it won't take long for learners to segment 'a + noun' as a determiner phrase in English with 'a' = indefinite (e.g., a dog, a cat, a student, a professor). It all depends on the input they are exposed to. And even after a few examples such as those here, learners are already beginning to do the following: 'Murphy' = noun, proper name, male = $[_{TP}$ Murphy]… and 'a' = determiner, indefinite, = $[_{DP}$ a]… boy' and 'boy' = noun, male, young, etc. = $[_{NP}$ boy]. So they are beginning to project syntax onto a sentence they are comprehending: $[_{TP}$ Murphy]$[_{DP}$ a $[_{NP}$ boy]]]. The verb may be missing, but it will be penciled in soon, and the VP will be projected into the sentences they hear. After all, if two- and three-year-olds can do this, why can't a 15-year-old or a 20-year-old?

The point is that the mind/brain comes equipped to handle language. Language simply has to be interpretable or comprehensible enough so the internal devices can do what they are wired to do. And you don't really have to "teach" anyone anything. The language-making device is ready to build phrases, find abstractions, and deal with the complexities in the input, as long as the learner can make sense out of what is said. We just have to give the language-making device time—the same time we give it in first-language acquisition—which means thousands of hours. Like Rome, language isn't built in a day.

References and Suggested Readings

You can actually read any "introduction to linguistics" book to see how complex language is, with all of its components interacting to create a sentence. You will also find information on how discourse adds another layer of complexity to understanding how language works. But here are several, one repeated from Chapter 2.

Burton, S., Dechaine, R., & Vatikiotis-Bateson, E. (2012). *Linguistics for dummies*. Mississaugua, Ontario: John Wiley & Sons. (I wouldn't normally recommend a book like this but this might be a good one to read before you read a hardcore linguistics text.)

Radford, A., Atkinson, M., Britain, D., Clahsen, H., & Spencer, A. (2009). *Linguistics: An introduction.* 2nd edition. Cambridge: Cambridge University Press.

It's very difficult to find accessible readings on sentence-processing and what linguists call *parsing* (sentence computation). However, to get an idea of how complex this issue is, I can recommend an older book:

Clifton, C., Jr., Frazier, L., & Rayner, K. (Eds.) (1994). *Perspectives on sentence processing.* Hillsdale, NJ: Lawrence Erlbaum Associates.

Think About It

1. Now that you have read this chapter, see if you can list the things that make language not just abstract but complex. Can you add a sentence or two for each item?

2. Using what you've read in this chapter, see if you can explain or illustrate this claim: *A language textbook can never capture the complexity that is language.*

3. Examine some books called "introduction" to language or "introduction" to linguistics. What topics do they cover? What does this suggest about the nature of language and all of the components that interact for us to comprehend and formulate sentences?

4. Following is a visual depiction of just four interacting elements in either the comprehension of or the production of a sentence. Can you explain this visual to someone else using ideas from this chapter about how different parts of language interact to form even a simple sentence?

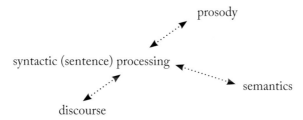

5. One issue that emerged in this chapter is how quick language processing is for native-speakers/listeners. The same can't be said for non-native speakers/listeners. Do you think non-native speakers ever get to the point of being as fast as natives at processing all the complex components when listening to a sentence? How do you feel about your ability to process sentences in another language?

6. If you were to distill the main idea of this chapter into a talking point, what would that be? How could you use that talking point to initiate a conversation with parents, administrators, colleagues, and others?
   If you engaged in conversation, what kind of example could you give to other people?

Chapter 4

Language is Implicit

What does 'implicit' suggest to you when you hear or read it? Everyday and dictionary definitions say something like "implied, hinted at, suggested," as in, "Maggie's question was an implicit criticism of the policies of this firm." In language and language acquisition we use the term a bit differently. 'Implicit' refers to something you cannot articulate or put into words. Remember the example of 'round'? You know 'round' when you see it, but you can't quite articulate what 'round' actually is. You have implicit knowledge of its meaning. In the language sciences we use 'implicit' almost the same way we might use 'unconscious' to refer to knowledge or representation you have that exists outside of your conscious ability to describe or articulate. We will see lots of examples in this chapter.

In this chapter, we will explore the idea that language—all language, even learner language in development—is implicit in nature. We know we have language—after all, we talk, sign, write, read, and so on—but we can't articulate its actual content, or we have great difficulty doing so. I recall at a dinner asking some non-linguists to tell me what the subject of a sentence was. I heard everything from "It's the thing the sentence is about" to "The thing that goes with the verb" to "The main noun." None of them could tell me what a subject was, but they all had a mental representation for it, or they couldn't understand or utter a basic sentence in any language. Their knowledge of the nature of 'subject' was implicit—and yours probably is, too, even if you're a teacher! You may think you have a definition of 'subject,' but a sentential subject is more abstract than what meets the eye.

Linguists, of course, attempt to describe language. As we saw in Chapters 1 and 2, those descriptions can get pretty abstract—and we only scratched the surface in those chapters. But even with linguists, sometimes the exact nature of a particular aspect of language eludes description. So let's look at some examples of the implicit nature of language. We will see that the implicit representation of language is not just "knowing" what something is but also the constraints and requirements on its participation in sentences.

An Example from English

Have you ever considered the nature of the most frequent word in English? I'm talking about the word 'the.' What is 'the'? Immediately you might say, "It's the definite article." Well, that's what we call it from the outside. But what is it, really? What's an article, and what does 'definite' mean? Let's look at some properties of 'the' to see just how much implicit representation you have for this little word.

Here's our first sentence: *The soldier ran the flag up the pole this morning.* Try to picture what this sentence is about. Now here's another: *The flag is a great symbol for any nation.* Is this as easy to picture as the first sentence? Probably not, partly because the phrase 'the flag' does not represent the same thing in this sentence that it did in the first one. In the first sentence, 'the flag' is a specific flag the soldier had in his or her possession. By all accounts, it is a "definite thing." But in the second example, 'the flag' is not any one flag, not a specific flag, but the *idea* of a flag. It is quite a different concept and not a "definite thing" as in the first example. Yet both phrases involve what everyone calls "the definite article." So what changes between the two sentences? Is it the meaning of 'flag'? The meaning of 'the'? Or a combination of the two? Either way, you have some underlying implicit notion of 'the' that lets you see that 'the flag' means two very different things in each sentence: one with clear "definiteness," one seemingly without.

Here's another example. What do you understand to be the meaning of 'the Russians' in each sentence that follow? Is the meaning the same? *The Russians are invading* versus *The Russians across the hall are having a party.* The first sentence refers to no specific Russians; we are not talking about Ivan, Boris, Masha and Olga. Instead, we mean Russians in general from the country of Russia, or maybe we mean the Russian government. In the second example, we talk about a small, particular group of Russians we know and can name. In this case, maybe their names are Boris, Ivan, Masha and Olga. So what makes 'the' definite when in one case we have a definite group and in another we don't?

Furthermore, as an English speaker you have underlying implicit knowledge that a word like 'the,' a word like 'this,' and a word like 'my' must all be syntactically related or similar. That is, they may have different meanings, but they have the same syntactic function. This is why in English you can't put two or more in the same sentence. Here are some examples:

The bike is rusted.
This bike is rusted.
My bike is rusted.
*The this bike is rusted.
*The my bike is rusted.

For those who speak Italian, I'm well aware that *la mia bicicletta* is possible. However, unlike Spanish *mi* and English *my*, *mia* in Italian is not a determiner but an adjective, and, because of how Italian works, *mia* raises to a position above the noun to give the standard Italian word order: *la mia bicicletta*. Note that Spanish also has *mia* as an adjective, but it can't raise *la bicicleta mia* vs. *mi bicicleta/*la mi bicicleta/*la mia bicicleta*, although the latter may sound slightly better to many speakers than the *la mi* combination.

Now let's contrast English and Spanish in a particular use of the "definite" article. When we talk about something generic, in English we use "bare nouns" without articles, as in *Dolphins are fun animals*. In Spanish, the exact same meaning is rendered with a definite article: *Los delfines son animales divertidos*. Both examples represent situations in which nothing definite is talked about; that is, no definite or specific dolphins. Yet Spanish requires a "definite" article, whereas English does not. So what makes a definite article, well, definite?

The point of this romp through 'the' is to show that, no matter what we choose to call 'the' from the outside, what it actually is and how it is used involves implicit knowledge within our representation of language. 'The' isn't so definite as we might think, but we have very good "ideas" about when to use it and when not to, regardless of whether something is "definite" or not.

> No matter what we choose to call 'the' from the outside, what it actually is involves implicit knowledge that is difficult to capture in words.

By the way, some languages, including Japanese and Turkish, have no articles—definite or otherwise. In Japanese, *Taroo ga ringo o tabemasu* can mean "Taro eats an apple", "Taro eats apples," or even "Taro eats the apple." Hmmm. What do definite articles do, then? The answer is that, ultimately, what definite articles are and how they function is really interesting only to linguists. We all have implicit knowledge about what they are, and why bother knowing the abstract and complex nature of these little words (unless you're studying linguistics)?

Before you go on...

Think about the last two sentences of the previous paragraph: "We all have implicit knowledge about what [definite articles] are, and why bother knowing the abstract and complex nature of these little words (unless you're studying linguistics)?" Do you think that knowing the abstract and complex nature of anything in language would help you teach something better? Do you think learners will acquire language better if they had access to this abstract and complex information in some explicit way? In what ways could knowing that language is abstract, complex, and implicit inform teaching?

An Example from Spanish

Every Spanish student learns early on that Spanish doesn't require subject pronouns. In a Spanish class, teachers tell students or students read in a textbook/online site that Spanish omits subject pronouns when it is clear who the subject is. So, for example, students learn that *hablo* ("I speak") is fine by itself and that *yo hablo* (also "I speak," but with a subject pronoun) is also fine. Every native speaker of Spanish knows this as well. But is there hidden and implicit knowledge about how subject pronouns work?

As you might guess, there is. For example, every speaker of Spanish as a first, second or other language comes to have implicit knowledge about restrictions on *overt pronouns,* or those pronouns we actually see and hear, such as *él* ("he"), *ella* ("she"), *ellos* ("they"), etc. When no pronoun is present, linguists have shown that a hidden pronoun called a *null subject* is there. In the sentence *Siempre hablo español con mi abuela* ("I always speak Spanish with my grandmother"), linguists have evidence of a hidden or null subject in the sentence. It's there, but you just can't see or hear it. Overt subjects you can see or hear. Let's look at an easy case, and then a more difficult case.

Every speaker of Spanish comes to know that overt subjects must have antecedents. No one teaches them this. They just come to know it implicitly. What does this mean? Let's look at English first. English requires subject pronouns in any simple sentence, or the sentence is ungrammatical. For example, you can't just say, "Speaks." You have to say, "Someone/he/she/Pablo speaks." Because English does not allow null subjects, this means that in expressions dealing with, say, weather and time, we insert what linguists call an "expletive" subject. In the case of weather and time, the expletive subject is 'it.' So "It's raining" and "It's three o'clock" are grammatical, while *"Is raining" and *"Is three o'clock" are not. "There" can also be an expletive subject, as in "There is an elephant in the room." You can't say *"Is an elephant in the room" as a declarative statement announcing the presence of a pachyderm.

Spanish allows for null subjects, which has numerous consequences; here are two. The first is that it prohibits expletive subjects. In Spanish, *Está lloviendo* ("It is raining") is grammatical, but *Él está lloviendo* is not. This is the opposite of English. Every speaker of Spanish comes to know this quickly and without being taught. Simultaneously, every Spanish speaker comes to know that an overt subject pronoun in the third person must have an antecedent. For this reason, a sentence like *Me robaron* is ambiguous, while *Ellos me robaron* is not. Both mean something like "They robbed me," but here's the difference. Only the first, without a subject pronoun, can be used when you don't know who

> There is implicit knowledge about how subject pronouns work in Spanish that all speakers receive, whether native or non-native.

robbed you. That is, if you enter your house and discover it's been ransacked and now your jewels and computers are missing, you call the police and say, *¡Me robaron!* This is because third-person null subject pronouns in Spanish don't require an antecedent. However, third-person overt subject pronouns do require antecedents. You can only say *Ellos me robaron* if you can name the people indicated by *ellos*; maybe Frank, Jimmy and Karen or your two cousins or those guys across the street. Because of this restriction on overt subject pronouns in languages like Spanish (and this is true of all null subject languages), you can't use expletive subjects like 'it' in weather, time, and other expressions. Such expressions have no antecedent or referent for the pronoun.

That's one aspect of implicit knowledge everyone grasps about Spanish subject pronouns without it being taught. But here's one that really gets into the weeds: overt subject pronouns not only must have antecedents but also are restricted on the kinds of antecedents they can take. Let's use this sentence in English as an example: "Not a single person said he was guilty." In this sentence, the antecedent of 'he' is ambiguous. It can mean some other person named Bob, Harry or Tim. It could refer to a defendant in a murder case. It could refer to a student accused of cheating. At the same time, the subject pronoun 'he' can also refer to 'no single person.' That is, no one in the room admitted his or her own culpability. (Side note: English can still use 'he' as the default genderless pronoun in spite of valiant efforts to un-gender the language.)

In Spanish, the overt subject pronoun él cannot do what English 'he' does. Spanish has two versions for the English sentence we just saw: *Ninguna persona dice que es culpable* and *Ninguna persona dice que él es culpable*. In the first version, the null subject pronoun can be interpreted as referring to "no single person" or to some other third person (Bob, Harry, Tim, the defendant, the accused student). However, in the second version, the overt subject pronoun él can only refer to some other third person, not to "no single person." The same holds when the antecedent noun is a *wh*-word or is modified by a *wh*-word, as in "Who says he is not guilty?" or "Which person says he is not guilty?" In Spanish, an overt subject pronoun cannot take these *wh*-elements as antecedents. Some of you Spanish speakers reading this might not have known this explicitly, but once you read this you said, "Yeah. That's right." This is because you have implicit knowledge (representation) about how null and explicit subject pronouns work. How did you get this implicit knowledge if you weren't taught it and didn't practice it?

By the way, not all subject pronouns are created equal; pronouns replace or stand in for a noun (or noun phrase). This definition works for third person in cases like "Linguistics is fascinating. But it can be a challenging subject." Here, 'it' stands in for 'linguistics' in the second sentence. But, as we saw above in weather expressions and other examples, 'it' does not stand in for anything (e.g., "It's raining" does not mean that 'it' is standing in for or replacing some previously mentioned noun). Moreover, what we call first- and second-person pronouns don't replace or stand in for anything, either. When I say, "I wrote this book," "I" doesn't replace any noun that preceded it. This stands in contrast to third person (e.g., "Chomsky wrote a book on language. In fact, he's written lots of books on language."). So there is much more to "subject pronouns" than meets the eye—and you have all this knowledge implicitly.

An Example from Japanese

Like many subject-object-verb languages (which, if you recall from Chapters 1 and 2, are actually head-final languages), Japanese has case marking. Because Japanese is head-final, the case marking comes after the noun, as in the following example (NOM = nominative, subject' ACC = accusative, object):

Taroo ga	*ringo o*	*tabemasu*
Taro NOM	apple ACC	eat

"Taro eats an apple"

Every student of Japanese learns about case marking, and it is readily apparent in the input that learners hear and see. However, under certain conditions, Japanese allows the optional deletion of case marking on the objects of verbs. So the above sentence could be *Taro ga ringo taberu*. Japanese does not allow the deletion of case marking on subjects so that **Taro ringo o taberu* and **Taro ringo taberu* are both ungrammatical.

However, under some conditions, deletion of the nominative case marker *ga* is permissible in spoken Japanese. These conditions involve abstract concepts involving the *verb class* (and according to some accounts, how "active" the noun is in the sentence). Verb class refers to whether or not the subject of the sentence originates within the verb (remember this from Chapter 2 and the examples from French as well as the verb *sink*?) and whether or not it is a *stative verb*. Stative verbs typically express a state, emotion, or mind-internal process. In such cases, whatever is expressed is viewed as static, without reference to change. Stative verbs include *can (be able), be, believe*, etc. In Japanese, *ga* deletion can occur with stative verbs. For example, both *Kami ga irimasu* and *Kami irimasu* ("Paper is necessary") are possible in spoken Japanese. In fact with some stative verbs, what looks like the object is actually marked with *ga*, not *o*. The dropping of case markers in Japanese have other complications that seem to involve discourse and pragmatics, but what we are laying out here is sufficient to let us know that the description of case marker deletion is complex and abstract, hence difficult to teach. Textbooks may note that case marker deletion is possible but do not make it clear exactly how it happens. It's just one of those things learners of Japanese are expected to "pick up." And when one examines the input, any clear-cut "rule" for case marker deletion can't be detected.

> Case marking deletion and the constraints on it are not taught. They're just something that learners are expected to "pick up."

Nonetheless, both L1 speakers and L2 speakers of Japanese do indeed wind up with implicit knowledge about how case deletion happens, what classes of verbs and kinds of case markers are involved, and other constraints on when case markers can be dropped, especially subject marker *ga*. (I've listed a reading at the end of this chapter for those who want to examine one study in particular.)

Before you go on...

Some people believe that implicit knowledge of language means being able to deploy language rules quickly and without thinking. Using language without thinking about it is a hallmark of fluency but not necessarily of mental representation. As we just saw with the example from Japanese, implicit knowledge of when to drop case marking includes when *not* to drop it. Imagine you only saw what a person "knows" through language use or communication. How do you know what that person knows to be both possible and impossible in a language? This is a valid question for both native and non-native speakers of a language. By the way, second-language learners demonstrate untaught knowledge of Japanese case marking during their second year of university language learning. How fluent do you think such learners are? Is it possible that we are often unaware of what learners "know" is possible and impossible only because we focus on what they produce?

Representation is Implicit All the Way

I am often asked questions such as "When does what learners learn in class become implicit knowledge?" or "How do learners develop implicit knowledge about the rules of the language?" I also hear, "How can I best assess my students' implicit knowledge?" I understand why people ask these questions, especially teachers. We are all trained to think that we study, we practice, so at some point language becomes implicit. But these questions miss the mark, because we know from research that implicit representation of language doesn't come from practice, but from exposure to communicatively embedded input coupled with internal mechanisms that organize and constrain language. Explicit knowledge does not become implicit knowledge. As I have tried to show, what we see on textbook pages isn't psychologically real. If such rules are not psychologically real, then how do they become anything?

> Implicit representation is present in all learners, even in beginners. Implicit knowledge is not just an end product to be found in advanced learners.

The question about when knowledge becomes implicit also contains the idea that an implicit representation for language is an edn-product. It is the result of of years of study and immersion, for example. While advanced speakers of a second language do have a good deal of implicit representation or knowledge of language, I challenge you to consider the following idea: *Implicit representation is present in less advanced learners, including beginners, intermediates, and levels in-between.* As teachers, we just don't look for it or don't see it as such, even when it is staring us in the face. Implicit representation is present all along, and what we see in development is an increasing move toward an implicit representation that is native-like. Let me say this another way: *Implicit representation of language begins at the outset but evolves over time.* We see this in syntax, for example, and morphology (verb endings, noun endings/markers, word formation, among other things), as well as the sound system and other domains of language. We'll look at two examples from the language I know best, Spanish. (I grew up with Spanish and English, so I have to keep coming back to my roots.)

Spanish has two verbs that are more or less equivalent to 'be' in function: *ser* and *estar*. Textbook rules, online rules, and teacher explanations describe some of the environments in which these verbs appear, but they don't really explain to students how these verbs work and why there are two. These verbs mostly have different functions: only *ser* can appear in sentences in which the predicate is a noun or noun phrase such as *Mi madre es doctora* ("My mother is a doctor"), and only *estar* is used as an auxiliary for progressives such as *Mi madre está examinando al paciente* ("My mother is examining the patient"). The issue of great consternation for teachers and learners is what happens with adjectives, because both verbs can be used with adjectives. People often rely on a rule of thumb that *ser* is used with adjectives that denote a permanent or inherent trait, whereas *estar* is used with adjectives when a condition or state is temporary. Anybody who teaches Spanish knows that this rule of thumb is fraught with problems immediately observable in *Kevin es muy joven* ("Kevin is young") and *¿Está muerta?* ("Is she dead?") Youth is temporary, and death is generally permanent. Something else is happening with these verbs—something deep and abstract—that governs how they interact with adjectives. (We won't review what that thing is, because it's not important to what we want to illustrate, but if you want a hint, it has to do with perfectivity, which we touched on in previous chapters. I've provided a reading for you at the end of the chapter if you wish to learn more.)

Research over the years has shown that learners of Spanish go through at least four identifiable stages in the acquisition of these two verbs. The research is based on spontaneous speech and elicited conversational speech in which chunks and formulaic expressions are removed, e.g., routines such as ¿Cómo estás? ("How are you?") which tend to exist as one unanalyzed chunk. For the record, we have data on both English and Chinese speakers learning Spanish, so the stages aren't due to first language influence; English has one verb *be,* and Chinese has none.

> Stage 1: No verb. Learners simply omit the verb, as in *Kevin joven* (lit: "Kevin young") and *María enferma* (lit: "Mary sick.")
>
> Stage 2: *Ser* emerges and takes over most functions of both verbs. *Kevin es joven* but also *María es enferma. Ella no es aquí* ("Mary is sick. She's not here"), *Paco es estudiando/Paco es estudiar* ("Paco is studying"), etc.
>
> Stage 3: *Estar* emerges as an auxiliary and learners gain control of its use with progressives as in *Paco está estudiando* ("Paco is studying").
>
> Stage 4: *Estar* emerges, and learners gain control over its use with location and with adjectives, as in *María está enferma* ("Mary is sick") and *Ella no está aquí* ("She's not here").

The research also shows that Stage 1 can be fleeting and quick (but doesn't have to be), while Stage 2 can last for some time. Stage 4 is particularly slow to emerge. and it takes considerable time for learners to gain control over this particular domain. In general, learners can take years to go through these stages in the acquisition of *ser* and *estar.*

So what does this all mean for the implicit nature of language in the learner's head? At every stage, the learner operates with an implicit representation of how tense is used in Spanish and what can be inserted to carry tense. Like English, the Spanish verbs for *be* are basically meaningless. They carry no real word-meaning compared to such verbs as *run, spit,* and *finish.* Spanish requires them to carry tense features (like English) and person-number features (unlike English, though *be* is irregular and has three forms in the present tense). In Stage 1, learners have yet to consistently project tense into the syntax, which is why we get sentences without copular (linking) and auxiliary verbs. This is consistent with learners' largely uneven ability to put person-number endings for present tense on verbs, often using "bare verbs" such as *corre* ("run") and *estudia* ("study") for most person-number situations (we'll see this in our second example in a minute).

Our conclusion is that Stage 1 here is implicit because (1) it does not resemble anything students are taught (who teaches them to leave out verbs?), (2) it does not resemble anything they practice (students practice putting verbs in, not leaving them out), (3) it does not resemble what's available in the input (regular sentences in Spanish always have verbs, and learners do hear, to some degree, different person-number endings), and (4) it does not look like English (so they aren't transferring a singular English *be* from the outset). Clearly they are not applying explicit or conscious rules. If they were, they would apply something like, "Okay, I can leave out the verb here."

The point is that their spontaneous and "free" output during communication (not classroom conversations where they are being "watched" or conversations in which they are monitoring their own performance) tends to reflect their implicit representation. We also see that implicit representation does not resemble anything going on in explicit instruction. Furthermore, every stage in the acquisition of *ser* and *estar* reflects abstract properties of language that are involved in the implicit nature of that stage.

Here's a second example (remember the present-tense paradigm for Spanish from Chapter 1? Here it is again for your convenience):

	SINGULAR	PLURAL
1ST	-o/ -oy	-mos
2ND	-s	-is
3RD	-a/-e	-n

To put the endings into something concrete, here is the verb *correr* ("to run") with these endings in the present tense:

	SINGULAR	PLURAL
1ST	corro	corremos
2ND	corres	correis
3RD	corre	corren

What does the development of verb forms look like in Spanish with second-language learners? We typically see the following in spontaneous and free communicative speech:

1. Learners use a bare verb, generally the same as third-person singular. This verb is "overgeneralized" to all person-number contexts (and even tenses).

2. The singulars emerge as learners gain control over them with third-person singular no longer being a bare verb only but actually being more and more restricted to third-person singular. Usually first-person singular emerges before second-person singular.

3. The plural forms emerge. Generally third-person plural that emerges before the others.

Clearly these stages do not reflect instruction or explicit practice. Instead, they represent what is happening in the implicit system from the outset. In Spanish, learners must develop a new functional phrase in the syntax labeled AGRP (Agreement Phrase). This phrase is nestled somewhere under the Tense Phrase so that the underlying structure (with all other functional phrases not present) looks like this:

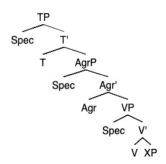

We won't get into the specifics here, but in Spanish, verbs will have to move out of their place of origin, pass through AGR, and wind up in T in regular declarative sentences. (We know this because of the various word orders in Spanish, and because we can test this with other languages similar and dissimilar to Spanish.) This is what learners are headed toward. But clearly in the initial stage, learners have no agreement. Their implicit system is, in essence, featureless when it comes to both Tense and Agreement. We might even characterize it as something like:

In other words, their initial representation is "bare bones." I'm not suggesting that this underlying structure is what is in the earliest stage of the implicit system (some scholars have claimed it is). What is clear is that learners are functioning with some kind of implicit system, or the first stage wouldn't be just bare verbs like *corre*. As in the case of *ser* and *estar*, this stage is not reflective of anything that learners are taught or learn explicitly. Moreover, though we call third-person singular "third-person singular," standard analyses concur that this particular verb form in Spanish is actually featureless. It is neither third-person nor singular. It basically doesn't indicate any person or number (though technically it does carry TENSE as a feature). Learners seem to have this implicit representation; that is, that something like *corre* is featureless. Therefore, it can be used in almost any context without "agreement clash." Our conclusion, then, is that they are working with an implicit system that does not resemble anything explicit they might know.

That the implicit system or representation is there all along often escapes us (especially those of us in world language teaching), because classroom students often engage in activities that direct their attention at some kind of accuracy. After all, even during "conversation," classroom learners know the purpose of such activities is to practice what one is learning in a public space where "how good they are" may be part of their identities. (In second-language research, we have "tricky" ways to tap into the implicit systems of learners, in addition to communicative and free output.)

> At any given stage, a learner's implicit system is not reflective of what learners are taught or have practiced.

One exception is what I hear from teachers who teach largely within a comprehension-based communicative classroom with no textbooks and little grammar instruction, or in ESL classes that focus less on learning rules and more on functioning in the surrounding world. Here, learners often freely express themselves with little monitoring. Spanish teachers engaged in comprehension-based teaching sometimes say, "Even though I use a variety of verb forms, why do my students seem to talk in the third person? How do I get them to use verb forms correctly?" Two things stand out to me when I hear such questions. The first is that in such classrooms, the implicit system is more observable because there is less emphasis on explicitly learning rules and paradigms. The second thing that stands out is that we have a long way to go to help teachers (as well as learners, administrators, parents, and others) understand the nature of language and its intersection with acquisition. After all, so-called "errors" are clear indications that the learner is developing an implicit system all along.

Before you go on...

Think for a moment about what we said early on in this book about patterns and rules as we compared them to constellations. Constellations are what we think we see, but in reality they don't really exist in real space. In what sense are many teachers seeing "constellations" in what learners do, not what is lurking underneath the surface in the learner's implicit representation or system?

Final Comments

In this chapter we have explored the idea that language as mental representation is implicit, no matter what explicit rules and descriptions we come up with. Although linguistics is a science that strives to figure out just what language is, linguists can and do disagree about some of the details. My training and education as a linguist has given me a particular perspective on language that happens to make the most sense to me and explains more about language than other perspectives with which I am familiar. So there are other ways to talk about language, yet they share the idea that language is implicit and is very difficult to describe in non-technical terms.

This is further evidence of just how implicit language is in our heads. We can't open our heads and look inside them. We can only observe how language "behaves" (i.e., what is both possible and impossible), and then linguists use methods of deduction to try to describe what they see. This is one reason why we wind up with such abstract, complex accounts of language. For example, when a linguist like me sits down and looks at something as simple as *yes/no* questions in Spanish and English, data emerge that are in need of explanation. Here are some examples:

> Bill reads books on syntax.
> Does Bill read books on syntax?
> *Bill lee libros sobre la sintaxis.*
> *¿Lee Bill libros sobre la sintaxis?*
> *Reads Bill books on syntax?
> (You can't invert subject and verb like Spanish.)
> *¿Hace Bill lee libros sobre la sintaxis?*
> (You can't insert *do* as in English.)

Seemingly, Spanish and English do different things, and without further scrutiny we might come up with "rules" such as "To make a *yes/no* question in Spanish, invert the subject and the verb" and "To make a *yes/no* question in English, insert a form of the helping verb *do* in front of the subject." But then the linguist sees sentences like the following, where the adverb and verb might be in different places in Spanish and English:

> Bill often reads books on syntax.
> *Bill lee a menudo libros sobre la sintaxis.*
> *Bill reads often books on syntax.
> (You can't separate a verb and its object with an adverb.)
> */?Bill a menudo lee libros sobre la sintaxis.*
> (Spanish usually doesn't like adverbs between subjects and verbs.)

Linguists like me might say, "Hmmm. Verbs are behaving in different ways in English and Spanish. They seem to wind up in different places in *yes/no* questions, declaratives, and when adverbs are present. I wonder what's causing this?" Then some more samples come along, like these (the critical sentences are the answers to the questions):

> Who's going to call Bill? Alessandro is going to call him.
> ¿Quién va a llamar a Bill? Lo va a llamar *Alessandro*.
> (Note that the subject in the second sentence appears after the verb.)

The linguist does another "Hmmm" and ponders that maybe something is unifying where subjects and verbs wind up in questions and in these different sentences. Then the linguist notices that some of the sentences in Spanish look the same in Greek, and there is also some overlap with French and German. How can this be? As that linguist goes deeper and deeper into the data, the abstract and implicit nature of language emerges.

Another major idea that we explored in this chapter is this: language is implicit for language learners as well as native speakers. Implicitness is not an end point; it's there all along. We saw how, even from the earliest stages of acquisition, learners create implicit representations that bear little resemblance to explicit learning and practice. So when teachers ask me, "How can I test my students' implicit knowledge?" my response is, "You probably don't want to, because it won't look like something you're interested in." That is, it won't look like the "internalization" of any rules the teacher is familiar with, and the implicit system is probably non-native-like.

This last comment may seem disconcerting to teachers and learners: *What good are textbook rules and paradigms, then, if learners are constantly creating something different from those rules?* That is a question I leave for you—but we will touch on it in the final chapter. For now I would like to say that language is a wonderfully rich human trait. We come equipped to acquire it; it just takes lots of time and patience. And just because we might question textbook rules doesn't mean we shouldn't have language classes—or even textbooks that look radically different from the ones currently out there. After all, students need exposure to language in communicative contexts. Who could do that better than a knowledgeable and patient teacher with good communicative and input-based materials to work with?

References and Suggested Readings

Some of the readings below contain technical information and jargon, but with just a bit of effort they are accessible.

Kanno, K. (1998). The status of a non-parameterized principle in the L2 initial state. *Language Acquisition, 5,* 317-335.

Schwartz, B. (1998). The second language instinct. *Lingua, 106,* 133-160.

VanPatten, B. (2010). Some verbs are more perfect than others: Why learners have difficulty with *ser* and *estar* and what it means for instruction. *Hispania, 93,* 29-38.

VanPatten, B. (2016). Why explicit information cannot become implicit knowledge. *Foreign Language Annals, 49,* 650-657.

Once more, just about any introduction to linguistics book will also give you a good glimpse as to the implicit nature of language.

Think About It

1. We've said that implicit knowledge is knowledge we can't articulate; we can't verbalize the content of implicit knowledge. Either we're not sure what that knowledge is, or we don't have the words to talk about it. Ask several people to define the following and see what happens. Can they verbalize their implicit knowledge? Where do they have difficulty? And how accurate are they in their definitions? And if they can, how many other abstract concepts do they embed in their definitions?

   - red
   - abstract
   - slippery
   - sky
   - language

2. Can you describe something about your non-native language for which you have a feel but can't quite put into words? (That is, you know that something sounds right or wrong in the language, but you're not sure why.)

3. Throughout this book, we have focused on language at the sentence level, often emphasizing sentences and morphology of words. Do people have intuitions and implicit knowledge about the sound system of their languages, either first or second? For example, in English we can reduce vowels to what we call a *schwa*. In the word 'constitution,' the second syllable 'sti' contains a schwa vowel. It sounds like 'uh,' though it's spelled with an 'i.' Does the average person know that the schwa exists? Can that person

explain the constraints or other factors related to when a schwa can appear and when it can't?

4. Toward the end of the chapter, we made the argument that at all stages of acquisition a learner's mental representation for language is implicit; a linguistic system doesn't need to be native-like for it to be implicit. What is your reaction to this idea?

5. In this chapter we have argued that the abstract and complex mental representation learners develop is present from the beginning. They develop it based on the communicative input they are exposed to. But could textbook rules be useful some other way? Consider this possibility: In the early stages, textbook rules help learners communicate—albeit in a controlled, non-native way—while their implicit systems build up in the background without them knowing it. At some point, these textbook rules "fade away" as the abstract, complex system takes over the process of language deployment during communication. What do you think of this possibility?

6. Related to Question 4 above is the concept of "errors." Teachers and others often talk about learners "making errors" and "what to do about errors." In what sense is the concern for errors part of the constellation metaphor? Do teachers see one thing but fail to notice what goes on behind the scenes? When teachers see errors, are they looking at what learners do from their own perspective, or from what the learner's internal implicit representation has in it?

7. What main idea(s) could you distill from this chapter as a talking point(s)? How could you use it/them to initiate conversations with parents, administrators, colleagues, and others? If you engaged in conversation, what kind of example could you give to other people?

Chapter 5

Talking Points

If you didn't already think that language for acquisition was special and different from other subject matter in schools and universities, then hopefully you do now. We ventured into the abstract, complex, and implicit nature of language—perhaps in ways many readers couldn't have imagined. And once again I feel the need to apologize to my fellow linguists for not always providing the full story, leaving out the details, and resorting to shortcuts. I deemed it necessary to keep certain things accessible and meet the promise of the subtitle of this book: *A Short Guide*.

Before we move on, let me once again be clear on this book's purpose. Many of us want language teaching to change. We want to do something other than having learners explicitly learn and practice textbook grammar and vocabulary, largely because language is not acquired this way. If indeed change is our goal (and it is mine), we need a way to talk to others about why we don't want to use the available textbooks or their methods, why we want new textbooks and materials. We must have arguments that what students are learning in such books isn't actually language, that language is something quite different. When we can make that argument, when we can convince other people that language is different from what they might believe, then we can take the next step regarding what we want to take place in classrooms. That is, for us to truly work toward communicative and proficiency-based language instruction for us to truly work toward language acquisition in the classroom, we must let go of our notions of language and convince others to do the same. Otherwise, educators may think that all teaching methods are about teaching "the same old thing." A truly novice method or approach, however, isn't teaching the same old thing at all if it truly focuses on communication and proficiency development.

In the spirit of keeping this book brief, this chapter will be shorter than most of the others, and will not end with additional readings or discussion questions. It really is a different kind of chapter. If it all works out, we will have a list of ways to engage in conversations about the nature of language and why language teaching must be special compared to other disciplines. I have found that the best way to get into discussions with people is to ask key questions. Let's start with goals.

Talking Point 1
What is the goal of language courses and language programs?

This question is a good conversation-starter. Most would answer, "To learn the language." My immediate question to that answer is, "What do you mean by 'learn'?" Almost everyone would state that a major outcome of language classes and programs is to be able to do something with language, to use it to speak, interact, engage other cultures, and so on. It's good to get everyone to agree on this goal, because then you can ask, "So if the goal is language use, why do we borrow so much from other disciplines to make language like other subject matter?" This can lead into a discussion of how textbooks treat language like subject matter to be learned, not language to acquire.

In addition—and this is especially true of university and college campuses with language requirements for degree programs—you might want to discuss why the language requirements are different from most other disciplines. For example, at many universities, the language requirement is the equivalent of four academic semesters. No other discipline in the university requires this amount of classroom time. Why do languages require more time? What are universities expecting by asking for a four-semester requirement? Secondary schools have similar situations: why do they have only one year of, say, biology but also have Spanish 1, 2, 3, 4, AP, and so on? This requirement has a hidden promise: time on task will lead to some kind of ability with, not knowledge about, language.

But there's more to bring up with the people you are talking with. So let's turn to the next talking point.

> **Before you go on...**
>
> Research some language programs at the secondary and university levels. How many of them state goals in terms of ability to use language? If so, what do the statements say? How many don't state any goals at all?

Talking Point 2

Most textbooks try to codify language in a way that can be taught explicitly, but I read recently that textbook rules and such aren't psychologically real. What do you think?

This question will inevitably lead to a discussion of what "psychologically real" means. This is where you can say, "Such rules don't exist in anyone's head. They're external descriptions of something too abstract to describe in everyday language." The person might ask what you mean by that. Now you can give an example from this book or from something else you've read. You can also bring up how linguists keep working to pinpoint the nature of language, so how could a textbook for French Level 1 do it?

People might be skeptical, so you'll need a few good examples up your sleeve. Convincing others that what's in textbooks bears little if no relationship to what winds up in someone's head is a tough row to hoe. Our constellation metaphor comes in handy here. Try talking to them about the Big Dipper, for example, and whether that constellation is "real" or just something we have imposed on what we see (see Chapter 1). This is always a good way to get people thinking. You can always say, "Even though we might not be able to describe what is really going on, we know that what we are seeing from the outside is not what's there." See if you can weave into the conversation that, if textbook rules are "real," then why don't they appear in courses in linguistics and the language sciences? Why do linguistic "rules" look so different from textbook "rules"?

Again, be prepared to offer one or two good examples of how textbook rules aren't real. In Chapter 2, we offered some ideas, and more can be found in the sources from the reading list for that chapter. You might consider offering some examples in English so that you can say, "Spanish, French, and

Japanese involve just as abstract notions as what we see in English." Here are several examples that don't appear in this book:

- *'That' deletion.* Have you ever noticed that we can delete 'that' as a clause complementizer, as in "I know that Bill is super cool" and "I know Bill is super cool." Here's another example: "Who did you say that Bill saw?" and "Who did you say Bill saw?" But note that we don't have two versions of "Who did you say claimed Bill is super cool?" because *"Who did you say that claimed Bill is super cool?" is not allowed. How does that deletion work in English? What governs it?

- *Subject position.* Have you ever noticed that in English it is the norm that subjects precede verbs as in "Bill drives to the gym" and "Bill writes a lot of books"? But, "On the corner is the post office" sounds fine, while "On the corner the post office is" doesn't. Then there are sentences like "Scarcely had I stepped out when my phone rang" and "No sooner had she read the email then she screamed" (but not *"No sooner she had read the email..."). And, of course, there are everyday occurrences such as "Here comes Murphy," while *"Here Murphy comes" doesn't sound so good. In contrast, "Murphy comes home late each night" and "Each night Murphy comes home late" are good sentences, but not *"Comes Murphy home late each night"/*"Each night comes home late Murphy." How do these word orders work? What governs them?

- *Consonant clusters.* Have you ever noticed that some consonant clusters appearing in word-initial position never appear in word-final position? For example, /dr/ in 'drama' is fine, but you can't find this sequence at the end of word. You can find /rd/ as in 'hard,' 'guard' and 'lard.' And you can't find /rd/ at the beginning of words, either. Other consonant clusters are allowed in both positions such as /st/: 'station' and 'static' as well as 'list' and 'mist.' What governs which consonants can cluster together and which ones can't in what part of the word?

Talking Point 3

Gosh, language seems so complex to me. Have you ever thought about what it takes for one little sentence to exist?

This is a great question for prompting people to think about how mind-boggling language really is. Try the sentence "Murphy's not here" from Chapter 3 on them, and ask them, "How many components must we juggle to comprehend and produce that simple sentence?" Through interaction with the other person's response, you can eventually get to the point where you've listed at least eight to ten things. Then you can ask, "Wow! How is it possible that this is ever learned by a student in our classes when we only focus on vocabulary and textbook grammar?" And you can follow up with "How do you think the two- and three-year old does it?" You should be able to steer the conversation slowly to the following: "We never teach students to juggle all of these things, yet they eventually do. Do you think the human mind is somehow equipped internally to do so?" This will lead to an interesting discussion in which you all ponder just what mechanisms must exist inside the human mind to work on language.

The idea behind this talking point is to get others to see that not only is what's in textbooks not psychologically real, but it isn't even the tip of the iceberg. Do we really think learners make some magical jump from the small amount of "rules" and "patterns" we provide them in textbooks to the dynamic and rapid-fire juggling of all the elements that go into making up a sentence? And if the learner eventually does this on his or her own, then what really did we do with our textbook rules and patterns?

Before you go on...

• • •

We often forget to talk about how first-language learners manage to juggle the complexity of language at such an early age with no teaching or intervention. Consider reading up on child first-language acquisition as background to how you discuss second-language acquisition. One good introduction is by Caroline Rowland, *Understanding child language acquisition,* published in 2014 by Routledge.

Talking Point 4

Do you ever stop to think about how much we know about language but have never thought about or can't articulate?

This question works best if you can do it with your conversational partner's second language. When you ask this question, you should receive an answer like "I don't follow you. What do you mean?" To that you can simply answer, "Well, we know far more than what we were taught or have been exposed to." You will probably be asked for some examples. Here are some quick, easy ones, followed by tougher ones. (And you can always ask them for the definition of 'round' if you want...)

- *'Re–' + verb.* Ask your interlocutor if "I repainted the walls" sounds like a good sentence to you. That person should say, "Yes." Then immediately ask, "What about 'I was tired so I reslept'?" That person should say, "No." Then ask, "How do you know this? Do you have a rule, or does it just sound wrong?" If that person claims to have a rule, ask for it, but it would likely be wrong. Be prepared with all kinds of different verbs to see if the person's rule works. These verbs are legit: *repaint, redo, rework, rearrange, reconsider, reseat, reheat, reinvent, reinvest, review, reclaim,* and *reignite.* These are not legit: *resleep, repet, rebake, reblink, respy, rerealize, relick, retaste, reswallow, regut,* and *renod.* (By the way, when you type these words, only the non-legit ones wind up being flagged by your spellchecker.) The discussion should lead to the idea that you have knowledge of how *re* + verb works that is unconscious and hard to articulate.

- *Objects can become subjects.* Ask you interlocutor what the difference is between a subject and an object. You'll probably get something like, "Subjects perform actions, and objects are acted upon." Then ask about passives: "In passives, don't objects become subjects? If so, how are they doing the action now?" Give an example, such as "The girl chased the dog" vs. "The dog was chased by the girl." This should lead to some interesting discussion. Then ask, "What about verbs like *sink, break,* and *melt*? I can say 'The captain sank the boat' but also 'The boat sank.' The boat was the object, and now it is the subject. And then there's 'Jimmy broke the window' and 'The window broke.' There's also 'I melted the butter' and 'The butter melted.' Seems like objects can become subjects, right?" The response should be, "I guess so." Here you add, "But what about something like 'I rode the bike'? I can't say 'The bike rode.' How about 'I drew the bath'? I can't say 'The bath drew.' So what do you think is going on with how objects can become subjects?" I can bet my car that you won't get a satisfactory answer unless you talk to a theoretical linguist. This means your final statement is, "We know so much about language. It's all implicit and unconscious. And we're not sure how it got there."

- *The impossibility of some contractions.* Ask your interlocutor what the verb is in this sentence: "John's happy." The response should be "is" or "be." Of course, that is the answer. "So we can contract 'is' 'am' and 'are' with subjects, right?" "Sure," the person says. And you can go through some examples together. "But can I say this in English: 'John's happier than Tim's.'" You should get a perplexed look; of course, you can't say that. You have to say the full verb with Tim: "John's happier than Tim is." "Interesting," your interlocutor says. You respond: "So what do you think allows us to contract the verb 'be' in some places but not others?" (Note that possessives are allowed at the end of a sentence, as in "John's got his book, and I have Tim's." So it's not just an end-of-sentence issue.) If you want to continue in this vein, you can say, "We can contract 'want to' to 'wanna' as in 'Do you wanna go?' and 'Who do you wanna take to the prom?' But I've noticed you can't contract 'want to' in sentences like 'Who do you want to tell John the bad news?' I mean, 'Who do you wanna tell John the bad news?' just sounds awful. Why do you think that is? How come I can contract in one place and not in another?" You can follow up with, "Oh, and here's another one. I can say 'I've done it' but I can't say 'Should I've done it?' Why not?"

This can lead to another example of just how much we have in our heads that we don't know we have and that the knowledge is implicit and unconscious.

Before you go on...

Many colleagues, parents, students and others believe that, through explicit practice, rules and patterns become implicit knowledge. How might you integrate this into your conversation and dispel this idea? One way is to show that explicit knowledge and implicit representation are qualitatively different things (Point 2 above is about this, and we have seen this repeatedly in this book). That is, abstract representation looks nothing like rules and patterns in textbooks. Another way is to show what development actually looks like (e.g., stages in the acquisition of something such as the example in Chapter 4: *ser* and *estar* in Spanish). Publications on second-language acquisition offer many examples.

These examples should guide you into some serious discussion about how implicit language works and that you wonder just what goes on in learners' minds that we don't normally think about or look for. If you're comfortable, bring up *staged development* and show how these stages must reflect something unconscious going on that is shaping language in the mind of the learner all along the way.

Talking Point 5

If language is abstract, complex, and largely implicit, can we really teach it like subject matter if our goal is acquisition or communicative ability?

This question should be brought up and discussed only after you've laid the groundwork with the other conversations suggested above. That is, think of this question as the goal question you eventually want to get to. You might get there in one long conversation with one colleague or parent or administrator, whereas with someone else you might need several conversations over time. The idea is that you can't anticipate what the other person will say, and you need to be patient if you want to lay the groundwork for a non-traditional pedagogy that doesn't treat language like other subject matter.

However, once you get there, it's a good time to ask the question, "I wonder what insights there are from acquisition that could inform a language pedagogy?" And that, my dear reader, is the conversation you've always wanted to have. This is the conversation in which the roles of communicatively embedded input, level-appropriate interaction, de-emphasis of explicit teaching and practice, and so on, come to light. Why can't you start with that conversation? Because the typical teacher, parent or administrator will almost always try to interpret a new methodology or pedagogy like old wine in new bottles; they will assume you mean that you want to teach the same old thing (textbook rules and patterns) in a new way. In their heads is this idea of textbook rules and prescribed vocabulary groups, and they think that is what you intend to teach with your new methodology. But is that what you mean? Hopefully not. You believe in a new pedagogy that is input-rich and communication-based, precisely because you understand language not to be what's in textbooks—and that language, because of its nature, can't be taught explicitly. You have to guide your listener to where you are before you can have the big "method discussion."

So who's been left out of this picture? *The learners in your classroom.* I often get the question, "How do you deal with those students who want to learn grammar and think that is what a class should be about? Those students who want worksheets and verb charts." The answer is that you deal with them the same way you deal with anyone else. Use these five talking points/questions to engage them. It is worth taking one day a week over five weeks to engage your students in this kind of discussion. I guarantee you they will be fascinated. And if you do it right, they will begin to look at textbooks and worksheets with a great deal of skepticism. And be sure to include measures such as focused can-do statements and other language-use "assessments" you all can point to and say "Hey! Look at what we can do now that we couldn't do two months ago."

Before you go on...

Districts and departments often want workshops on teaching and what happens in classrooms. As we have argued, this puts the cart before the horse. That is, professionals need to engage in serious discussion about the nature of language *(cont.)*

(and, for that matter, the nature of communication) before they can talk about acquisition and teaching. How might you convince your colleagues or administrators that a professional development workshop or two on the nature of language would be a good idea?

Some Final Thoughts

As you can tell, this book is not about acquisition or language teaching, even though occasionally we touched on both. It's certainly not a "how to" book—there are lots of those around. Instead, it is a "why" book. In my experience, we just don't spend enough time talking about one of the "whys," which is one reason why language teaching hasn't changed much since the onset of the acquisition era and the accompanying communicative revolution of the early 1970s. It is also one reason why new methods are misunderstood, distorted, and why they tend to die out. The input-rich, communication-centered classroom is doomed to fail if the teacher thinks she is teaching rules and patterns but her students show no evidence of having learned these things "right away" as in a traditional method. So the "whys" are as vital as the "hows." You can't have one without the other.

I want to close by revisiting constellations, a recurring theme in this book. Hopefully you remember what was discussed in Chapter 1: constellations are an illusion. They are patterns we impose on a seemingly flat sky. Yet we know space is not flat; from another point in space, any given constellation would be unrecognizable. In essence, constellations disappear once we get far away enough from Earth and out into the vast universe. Moreover, in a billion years stars and galaxies will have shifted from current positions as the universe continues to expand. So future earthlings looking up at the night sky will not see Orion, Scorpio, or the Big Dipper—at least not the way we see them now. Constellations are inventions of ancient imaginations, yet to this day we look at them the way our ancestors did.

At the same time, space and the universe aren't illusions. Stars and galaxies aren't illusions. There is something out there. We get glimpses of it when we look up at night. We constantly discover many things about space and how it works, what its relationship is to time and gravity, what the universe may or may not look like in ten billion years, and what actual laws govern the structure of space-time. We know now that the way we once thought of the universe is not what it actually is.

Finally, although we know some things, there are other things we just don't understand yet—and physicists are still trying to reconcile relativity with quantum mechanics, for example. Language is like that, too. Although we presented some ideas in this book about the nature of language, because linguists have been working at it for some time, explanations about what we "see" with language may change. But there is something constant: without looking deeper into what language really is, it will remain an illusion—an invention of our imaginations—if we focus on surface "patterns."

We must keep in mind that, ultimately, language is abstract, complex, and implicit. Those characteristics will never change, no matter how linguistic theory is modified or how theorists talk about language. And those fundamental characteristics should inform how we fashion acquisition-oriented, communicative, proficiency-based classrooms. We know people can acquire language; we just need to leave it to the human faculty for acquisition to let language be whatever it is. We must stop making language something it isn't.

Epilogue

The original draft of this manuscript did not have an epilogue. On reflection, I thought an epilogue might be a good place to address several issues that don't quite fit into the body of the book, largely because this is not a "how to" book about language teaching but a book about the nature of language, aimed mostly at language educators. However, I often hear about these issues. You can, of course, skip this epilogue and not be worse off. But because it's here, and some of the issues it raises may be interesting, I invite you to read on. And guess what: the epilogue is short.

One person read Chapter 4 and said that the book implies that all classroom activities that have been designed to help students master language structures are well-meaning but a waste of time. There's research that supports that contextualized grammar instruction, supported by corrective feedback and the opportunity to notice input features, is effective.

This is correct. Based on what I've written here, there is the implication that classroom activities designed to promote mastery of structure are a waste of time *regarding language acquisition*. Mastery of structure makes sense only if you believe language is something other than an abstract, complex, implicit system. If you believe that textbook rules are real or somehow "turn into" the abstract, complex, implicit system, then this position makes sense. I would argue the opposite: no evidence suggests that explicit teaching and practice lead to anything other than explicit learning (more on this in a moment). The research that is there just isn't compelling, for a variety of methodological reasons; that is, research methodology and experimental design.

Furthermore, most major theories used in L2 research put (severe) limits on the effects of explicit learning and so-called "mastery." Here's one source, so you can see just how most theories address this issue: a book called *Theories in Second Language Acquisition,* edited by Jessica Williams and myself, published in 2015 by Routledge. (A third edition will come out soon, for which the editors have changed to Bill VanPatten, Gregory D. Keating, and

Stefanie Wulff.) Not all of the contributors overlap 100% in how they address the issue of focusing learners' attention on grammar in some way, but if you read carefully, you will see that most put limits on what such efforts actually do or can do.

Moreover, those working from a psychological perspective are beginning to converge on the central idea that second-language acquisition is largely implicit in nature. Acquisition of an abstract, complex linguistic system does not happen because of explicit teaching and practice. For a good volume on this, see *Implicit and Explicit Learning of Languages,* edited by Patrick Rebuschat, published in 2015 by John Benjamins Publishing.

After some fifty years of research, we can make only one real conclusion about this kind of research: explicit teaching and learning leads to explicit knowledge of some kind, not to abstract, complex, and implicit knowledge.

For the reader wanting some names to look up on this (to make sure it's not just BVP saying this), here are some who would (largely) agree with my position: Roger Hawkins, Michael Sharwood Smith, John Truscott, Cathy Doughty, Maria Pavesi, Teresa Pica, Manfred Pienemann, Michael Long, Stephen Krashen, Bonnie Schwartz, and many others. This book is not the place to review this research, and I refer readers to a new book Megan Smith, Alessandro Benati and I have written that will appear soon with Cambridge University Press, *Key Questions in Second Language Acquisition: An Introduction.* (In Chapter 6, we review this line of research.)

Another comment I often hear goes something like: "Generative linguistics has nothing to offer teachers. Why should we bother?" This statement is true, and the answer to the question is, "Don't bother *if and only if you believe that textbook rules or some other kind of rules are psychologically real.*" But here's my preferred answer. Many language educators are always looking for one of two things: (1) new ways to teach the same old thing (established grammar concepts and vocabulary), and (2) some new insight into language that will better help them explain language to students. My reaction to this is, "I get it. I totally understand why teachers want such things. After all, they've been trained to look for them." But in generative linguistics—and linguistic theory, more generally—what we find is not a new way to teach the same old thing or new ways of explaining something. Instead, we find the best explanation for considering not doing the same old thing at all! And that is the purpose of this book. As Chapter 5 lays out, knowledge about the abstract, complex, implicit nature of language can provide arguments for teachers who want to abandon the old and try something truly different. Of course, so does knowledge about acquisition—but that would be a different book. My point is that generative linguistics has much to offer language teachers in the realm of not *what*, but *why you might want to explore other options*.

Generative linguistics, along with an understanding of how acquisition works, helps us to understand just why the same old teaching of grammar and vocabulary does not directly or indirectly affect acquisition. My aim is to help teachers move beyond looking for what kind of grammar and vocabulary to teach and instead to embrace communicative, proficiency-based language teaching that is truly acquisition-oriented. To be sure, there's no one way to do this, but that's what makes language teaching so exciting and fun: we get to explore and try things out. And it also provides new territory for publishers and materials developers. It's a tough row to hoe; I've been working at it for three decades, and, as you can tell, I haven't given up on it.

So, yes, a book like this will not give you something to teach on Monday morning. My hope is that it will be food for thought about why you might want to do something different next year.

About the Author

Bill VanPatten, Ph.D. (University of Texas), has had a long, distinguished career in language acquisition and language teaching. He has held positions at the University of Illinois at Champaign-Urbana, the University of Illinois at Chicago, Texas Tech University, and most recently Michigan State University. He has published eight books, eight edited volumes, five college-level textbooks in Spanish and French (including movies and one telenovella for students), more than 130 articles and book chapters, and stories and fiction for students of Spanish. He is a frequently invited guest speaker and has lectured around the world. He was the host of *Tea with BVP*, a call-in talk show for language teachers, and now hosts its follow-up show, *Talkin' L2 with BVP*. When not engaged in such endeavors, he writes fiction. His debut novel is *Seidon's Tale*.